MICROWAVE ENTERTAINING

Marcia Cone
& Thelma Snyder

Photographs by Rita Maas

SIMON AND SCHUSTER
New York   London   Toronto   Sydney   Tokyo

ALSO BY THE AUTHORS:
Microwave Diet Cookery
Mastering Microwave Cookery
The Microwave French Cookbook
The Microwave Italian Cookbook

SIMON AND SCHUSTER
Simon & Schuster Building
Rockefeller Center
1230 Avenue of the Americas
New York, New York 10020

DESIGNED BY BARBARA MARKS
Manufactured in the United States of America

10 9 8 7 6 5 4 3 2 1

Library of Congress Cataloging in Publication Data

Cone, Marcia.
  Microwave entertaining/Marcia Cone & Thelma Snyder;
photographs by Rita Maas.
    p. cm.
  1. Microwave cookery. 2. Menus. I. Snyder, Thelma. II. Title.
TX832.C67   1989
641.5′882—dc20   89-37839
                                                    CIP

ISBN 0-671-62548-9

To
Koji
and
Dave,
our
partners
in
entertaining.

We'd like to thank all those who made this book possible and cared for it as their own: Carole Lalli, our editor; Kerri Conan, her assistant; Barney Karpfinger, our agent; and the photography team of Rita Maas, food stylist Diane Elander, and prop stylist Susan Byrnes.

CONTENTS

Introduction
11

THE MENUS

INTRODUCTION

THOUGHTS ON ENTERTAINING

Recently we read a magazine devoted to entertaining and couldn't help but notice that nearly every party involved some sort of outside help such as a catering service. The one exception, a dessert gala, demanded tremendous culinary skill, lots of time, and a fat wallet. We wondered if there is a place in this world of sophisticated palates for the individual who merely wants to "show hospitality," which is Webster's definition of *entertain*.

For most of us, giving a party can be nerve-racking; it means opening up our homes, our food preferences, and our cooking abilities to the scrutiny of others. Would anyone but the most confident host (or one with a tried-and-true caterer) subject himself to this?

We hope that with this book you'll gain another perspective on entertaining. It is possible to reduce time and effort without sacrificing quality. You can have guests come to your home for food and drink, even if you are chronically short of time. And a special evening together can revolve around something as simple as meat loaf and wine.

Although this is a microwave entertaining book, it is not strictly a collection of recipes for the microwave oven. The microwave oven is an appliance that should be used in conjunction with all the other appliances in the kitchen. Here the conventional stove top is summoned into service to fry Indian vegetable pancakes, or the grill to finish off a juicy Cornish hen. The menus are designed to make the most of your tools and energies.

But, as all who own one know, the microwave oven has definite advantages, and the obvious one is time savings—in preparation and actual cooking as well as in last-minute reheating. At the same time, you will find that all of our recipes have been specifically tailored for microwave cooking and many can't be duplicated as well conventionally. For instance, there are vegetables simmered in their marinade, steamed pumpkin and raspberry breads, fish fillets cradled and cooked in mounds of nutmeg-scented spinach, and even a down-home meat loaf, mixed, cooked, and served on the same platter.

This book is a collection of our favorite dishes—the ones requested over and over again by our family and friends—cheesecake, chocolate bread pudding, veal daube, and others that have simply evolved with the changing food trends.

When it comes to entertaining, people naturally have different styles. Some prefer the solid, dependable, and convivial, such as meat loaf and chili, and feel more comfortable with a table setting of pottery plates, chunky bistro glasses, and wooden salt bowls. But there are others who love fine linen spread with hand-painted china and cut glass, and who feel that having people in their homes is more special than going out to fancy, overpriced restaurants. For others, most of us perhaps, both approaches appeal, depending on the occasion.

If you aren't already confident of your personal entertaining style, there are questions to ask yourself that will help decide the atmosphere you want to create. Think about your favorite restaurant, café, or coffee shop—what sort of mood does it set to make you feel comfortable? Perhaps it is the music, the crisp linen napkins, the copper bowls full of flowers, the intimate tables, the aromas that greet you, or a charmingly lighted painting. It is possible to simulate any or all of these mood elements in your home or apartment. And remember that even your old, tired room will look better to you if you rearrange it a bit, and it will always look inviting to your guests.

Whatever your style, there are some basic questions you should ask yourself before you embark on a menu. You'll find them in the sidebar on the next page.

The thirty menus that follow have been compiled according to our tastes and according to what dishes we feel work together food- and timewise. We've worked out a preparation plan for each menu to help you get all the dishes on the table in a reasonable order. The recipes for each menu should be read very carefully before the preparation plan is followed—to avoid mistakenly heating things twice, etc., and for efficient execution of the meal. This time grid reflects food-preparation time; we didn't build in time for setting the table, dressing, or last-minute cleanups, so make your own adjustments. But do follow the plan for the most efficient execution of each dinner. Depending on how formal we want to be, we like to set up the table at least a day or two in advance to decide on plates, serving platters, and table decoration. Coffee cups, spoons, creamers, etc., can be set up on trays away from the kitchen activity but all in one place when you need them.

A word about wines: We are not experts, though we do enjoy the interplay between food and wine and the experimentation involved in finding a good match. But keep in mind that there isn't just one wine or even type of wine that might be right with a particular dish. Because there are so many complex flavors in contemporary dishes (herbs, exotic fruits, wild mushrooms, etc.), the rule is no longer red wine for meat and white wine for fish. The choice often comes right down to personal taste, and which characteristics of the food you might like to emphasize. Of course, the most professional way to make a choice would be to pretaste the main dish with at least a couple of wines, but if you don't have the time or the inclination for that, we give wine suggestions to serve as your guide.

We have planned the menus with the notions of contrast and complement—in flavor, texture, color, and mood—in mind. We also offer options, usually for the sake of even greater efficiency but sometimes simply for variety, particularly in the dessert course. We hope that our suggestions will inspire you to find far more than thirty menus among the one hundred or so recipes in this book.

ENTERTAINING QUESTIONS

❡ *How many can you serve? This is not the same as how many you want to serve. An elbow-to-elbow party can be as successful as one where people are seated comfortably, but make sure that you have the dishes to accommodate the menu, the room is adequately ventilated, and so on.* ❡ *What plates and serving dishes will you need? If you plan to serve soup, make sure you have enough bowls or soup dishes—but they don't need to all match. Food can and should be chosen to complement the serving pieces, so paint a picture in your mind before you begin.* ❡ *Would a buffet or sit-down dinner be better?* ❡ *What do you want to serve: a full dinner, just dessert or appetizers? If a full dinner, will you serve all the courses in the same room?* ❡ *What season is it? Try to plan according to what products are at their peak. Be flexible.* ❡ *How much time will you have for advance cooking? Be realistic (that is why we provide "Even Easier Hints" with each menu). Consider take-out appetizers or store-bought desserts if you simply don't have time.* ❡ *What day do you want to entertain? Sunday is a great day for brunches or dinner. If you work outside the home, this probably will mean you will have an extra day to prepare.* ❡ *What do you know about your guests' food tastes? Do they have any strong dislikes or allergies?* ❡ *Think about the wines in terms of the specific dishes they will be served with as well as the overall menu, especially if more than one wine is to be served.* ❡ *If budget is a concern, add up the costs of everything—wine, flowers, and food—to avoid unpleasant surprises. Deciding what is an acceptable cost per person can help.*

SUGGESTED UTENSILS

DISHES:

All dishware should be made of heatproof glass (to withstand the heat of the food while it is cooking), without any metal trim. Plastic cookware should be marked with a suitable-for-microwave seal.

1-quart covered casserole
2-quart covered casserole
3-quart covered casserole
4-quart covered casserole
1-cup glass measure
2-cup glass measure
4-cup glass measure

8-cup glass measure
10-inch Pyrex pie plate
9-inch Pyrex pie plate
2-quart rectangular baking dish
9-x-5-inch loaf pan
8-ounce oval ramekins

Individual cook-and-serve dishes made of glass or ceramic with nonmetallic trim:
    10-inch dinner plate
    12-inch round plate
    1½-cup soup bowl or mug
    6- or 7-ounce custard cups

Large Pyrex mixing bowl
12-ounce cereal bowls
8½- or 9-inch Pyrex cake plate

EQUIPMENT:

Ice cream scoops:
    large (¼ cup)
    small (⅛ cup)
7-inch serving plates
    (to make the food seem like more)
Food processor or blender
Parchment paper

TERMS

COVERING:

"Cover tightly" means to cover with a casserole lid or plastic wrap that has been folded back slightly on one side.

"Cover with wax paper" means to lay the wax paper loosely on top of a dish.

When paper towel is indicated as a cover, any toweling will work as long as it has been manufactured for kitchen use.

If no term is mentioned in the recipe this indicates that a cover is not necessary.

POWER SETTINGS:

HIGH is full power for your oven.
MEDIUM will be 50 percent (5) on a full-powered oven or about 70 percent (7) on a smaller, lower-powered oven.
DEFROST will be 30 percent (3) on a full-powered oven or about 50 percent (5) on a smaller, lower-powered oven.
LOW will be 10 percent (1) on a full-powered oven or 20 percent (2) on a smaller, lower-powered oven.

COOKING TIMES:

There will be a range of cooking times, because ovens vary in cooking power from 400 to 750 watts. The lower the wattage, the longer the cooking time, particularly on HIGH power. Most lower-powered ovens adjust their middle-power ranges to be about equal to larger ovens (see above). You may even notice a difference in cooking times throughout the day, depending on the power output in your home at any given time. Begin with the lowest times until you know where your oven falls in the time range.

MICROWAVE ENTERTAINING

CONNECTICUT SUMMER TROUT DINNER

Serves 4

Silver Queen Corn Custard
with Herbed Mushrooms

Lake Trout with Lemon-
Walnut Butter

Warm Garden Tomato
Slices with Basil

Fresh Bakery Rolls with
Pepper Jelly

Warm Three-Berry Sauce
for Ice Cream or Sherbet

Chocolate Leaf Cups

Serves 4

Silver Queen Corn Custard
with Herbed Mushrooms

Lake Trout with Lemon-
Walnut Butter

Warm Garden Tomato
Slices with Basil

Fresh Bakery Rolls with
Pepper Jelly

Warm Three-Berry Sauce
for Ice Cream or Sherbet

Chocolate Leaf Cups

WINE SUGGESTION
Chardonnay from the Haight
Vineyard, Litchfield,
Connecticut, or California
Chardonnay

T his menu, for mid to late summer, was inspired by the local foods from Litchfield County, Connecticut, where Thelma grew up and still spends much time foraging for fresh-food ideas. "Fresh lake or brook trout, wild greens, vine-ripened tomatoes, Silver Queen (a white corn grown near the Bantam Lake area), and wild berries are foods we dreamed about in the depths of winter. Homemade rolls are a touch my mother would have added, but a good bakery roll will be a more than adequate vehicle for the pepper jelly." ❦ There is no appetizer with this menu, but instead a first-course savory custard. A main course of trout is presented on the same plate with tomatoes, followed by dessert. All those wonderful outdoor flavors are combined in a tantalizing but simple menu.

PREPARATION PLAN

THE DAY BEFORE:

1. Make the Chocolate Leaf Cups and refrigerate.
2. Make the Pepper Jelly and refrigerate.

AT LEAST 1¼ HOURS IN ADVANCE:

1. Butter and crumb the custard cups and mix up the corn custard mixture.
2. Cut up the mushrooms for the corn custard's sauce.
3. Prepare the tomato slices for cooking.
4. Assemble the fish and sauce in their respective cooking dishes.
5. Wash the berries and measure out the ingredients for the rest of the sauce.

½ HOUR BEFORE SERVING:

1. Pour the corn custard into the prepared cups and cook.
2. During the standing time of the custards, cook the mushrooms for the sauce. Serve as the first course.

AT THE TABLE:

1. While clearing the custard plates, cook the trout.
2. During standing time of the trout, cook the tomatoes.
3. Arrange the fish on serving plates and spoon on the sauce. Garnish with parsley and serve.

TO SERVE DESSERT:

While preparing coffee and/or tea, heat the berries in their sauce. Scoop out the ice cream or sherbet onto the chocolate leaves, then top with the berry sauce to serve.

EVEN EASIER HINTS

1. Eliminate the Chocolate Leaf Cups and pass a good-quality chocolate-mint wafer.
2. Substitute unsalted butter or Parsley Butter (see page 22) for the Pepper Jelly.

CUTTING CALORIES

For an elegant but more calorie-conscious menu, eliminate the ice cream and Chocolate Leaf Cups from the dessert and serve only the berries. Give them a bright country flavor with a light grinding of black pepper and a splash of Raspberry Vinegar (see page 42).

SILVER QUEEN CORN CUSTARD WITH HERBED MUSHROOMS

Serves: 4

Cooking time: 12 to 19 minutes

3 tablespoons unsalted butter

¼ cup fine dry bread crumbs

2 ears fresh white corn, shucked, or 1 cup
frozen kernels, thawed

8 reserved inner leaves from corn husk,
for garnish (optional)

3 large eggs, beaten lightly

1 teaspoon cornstarch

¾ cup half-and-half

1 teaspoon sugar

¼ teaspoon salt

¼ teaspoon cayenne pepper

⅛ teaspoon freshly ground black pepper

½ cup grated Monterey Jack or Muenster
cheese

2 tablespoons chopped fresh chives

1 pound mushrooms, cut into ¼-inch
slices

1 tablespoon chopped fresh parsley

1 teaspoon fresh lemon juice

12 chive tops, cut into 3-inch lengths, for
garnish

Divide 1 tablespoon of the butter among four 5- or 6-ounce ramekins or custard cups, and butter the insides well. Divide the bread crumbs among the ramekins, sprinkling to coat them well. Set aside.

With a serrated knife, cut the corn kernels from the cobs into a 2-cup glass measure; with the back of the knife, scrape the remaining corn from the cobs into the same bowl. (There should be about 1 cup.) Reserve inner leaves for garnish, if desired. Add 1 tablespoon of the butter. Cover with wax paper and cook on HIGH for 2 to 3 minutes or until the butter is just melted.

In a large bowl, combine the eggs and cornstarch and whip with a whisk until smooth. Add the half-and-half, sugar, salt, cayenne, black pepper, cheese, 1 tablespoon of the chopped chives, and the corn-butter mixture. Stir until well blended. Divide the mixture among the four prepared ramekins. Place the ramekins 1 inch apart in the microwave oven. Cook, uncovered, on MEDIUM for 10 to 14 minutes or until the custards are firm and a knife inserted close to the center comes out clean, rearranging the cups if necessary after 5 minutes.

Let the custards stand for 5 minutes. In the meantime, place the remaining 2 tablespoons butter, the remaining 1 tablespoon chives, the mushrooms, parsley, and lemon juice in a 2-quart microwaveproof casserole. Cook, uncovered, on HIGH for 2 to 4 minutes, stirring after 1 minute or until just tender.

To serve, run a thin knife around the edge of each ramekin, and turn the custards out onto individual serving plates. Spoon the mushroom sauce around the outside of each custard and garnish each with 3 chive tops.

LAKE TROUT WITH LEMON-WALNUT BUTTER

Serves: 4

Cooking time: 14 to 22 minutes

As children, we used to collect walnuts in the backyard, and during the long winter months, we would open them and store them in jars for mother's cooking, or just for eating.

Place the fish on a 3-quart rectangular microwave-proof dish or oval plate with the tail ends toward the inside of the dish. Cover the eyes with a strip of smoothly folded aluminum foil. Sprinkle with 2 tablespoons of the lemon juice. Cover tightly with the lid or plastic wrap turned back slightly on one side and cook on MEDIUM for 12 to 18 minutes or until the fish flakes when pressed with the finger. Let stand, covered, for 5 minutes before serving.

Meanwhile, place the butter and walnuts in a 4-cup glass measure. Cook on HIGH for 2 to 4 minutes or until the butter is melted. Stir in the remaining ¼ cup lemon juice, the chopped parsley, lemon rind, salt, and pepper. Stir until well mixed.

To serve, place one fish on each plate and remove the foil. Spoon the sauce over the fish. Place a whole parsley leaf over each fish eye.

NOTE: A small amount of foil, wrapped smoothly around the food (with no sharp edges sticking up) and not touching the sides of the oven will not damage your oven.

4 whole trout (6 to 8 ounces each),
    cleaned and trimmed
¼ cup plus 2 tablespoons fresh lemon
    juice
½ cup unsalted butter
1 cup coarsely chopped walnuts
½ cup chopped fresh parsley
1 teaspoon grated lemon rind
½ teaspoon salt
½ teaspoon freshly ground black pepper
4 whole parsley leaves

WARM GARDEN TOMATO SLICES WITH BASIL

Serves: 4

Cooking time: 2 to 3 minutes

4 firm ripe tomatoes (each about 3 inches in diameter), or 16 small pear or cherry tomatoes
3 tablespoons olive oil
¼ cup fresh basil, stems removed and cut into thin strips
Freshly ground black pepper

Remove the tomato stems and cut the tomatoes crosswise into ¼-inch slices, or cut small tomatoes in half. Arrange the slices in an overlapping circle around the edge of a 12-inch microwaveproof platter. Drizzle the slices with the olive oil. Sprinkle with the basil and pepper. Cover with wax paper and cook on HIGH for 1½ to 3 minutes or until the slices are just heated through. Place on serving plates next to trout.

PARSLEY BUTTER

Makes: ½ cup

Cooking time: ½ minute

½ cup unsalted butter
¼ cup minced fresh parsley
Dash Tabasco

Place the butter in a small microwaveproof bowl. Heat on DEFROST for 30 to 45 seconds or until softened but not melted. With a spoon, mix in the parsley and Tabasco. Spoon into a crock and refrigerate to chill.

PEPPER JELLY

Makes: 5 cups

Cooking time: 9 to 15 minutes

2 medium-size green peppers, stems and
    seeds removed
4 to 5 jalapeño peppers, stems, seeds, and
    ribs removed (the seeds and ribs will
    add more fire!)
5 cups sugar
1 cup cider vinegar
Few drops green food coloring
6 ounces liquid pectin

This is delicious as a dip for pretzels or on cream cheese and crackers with drinks, especially Margaritas. It is a perfect condiment with grilled fish and meats. Batches of hot green jalapeño and sweet red pepper jelly make lovely hostess gifts at Christmas. Try the sweet variety on warm dinner rolls.

Finely chop or process the green and jalapeño peppers. In a 3-quart microwaveproof casserole, combine the chopped peppers and the remaining ingredients except the pectin. Cook, uncovered, on HIGH for 8 to 12 minutes, until the mixture comes to a full boil. Stir well to make sure that all the sugar is dissolved. Stir in the pectin.

Cook on HIGH for 1 to 3 minutes or until the mixture comes to a boil. Stir well and spoon or pour the mixture into sterilized jars. Cover tightly. Store in the refrigerator for up to 4 months.

Variation:

SWEET PEPPER JELLY: Substitute 3 or 4 sweet red peppers (eliminate the jalapeño peppers), and red food coloring for the green.

WARM THREE-BERRY SAUCE FOR ICE CREAM OR SHERBET

Serves: 4 to 6

Cooking time: 3½ to 5 minutes

2 tablespoons unsalted butter
½ cup raspberry preserves
1 tablespoon Framboise or Triple-Sec
2 cups mixed fresh berries
1 pint vanilla or French vanilla ice cream,
or fruit sherbet

We prefer to make this with a combination of strawberries, raspberries, and tiny wild blueberries, but any combination will be delicious.

In a 4-cup glass measure or 1-quart microwaveproof casserole, combine the butter, preserves, and liqueur. Heat on HIGH for 1½ to 2 minutes or until the butter is melted and the preserves are bubbling. Stir well. Fold in the fresh berries. Heat, uncovered, on HIGH for 2 to 3 minutes or until just heated through. Spoon the sauce immediately over scoops of ice cream or sherbet nestled in the Chocolate Leaf Cups.

CHOCOLATE LEAF CUPS

Makes: 4 cups

Cooking time: 2 to 5 minutes per cup

12 ounces semisweet chocolate pieces
4 attractively shaped cabbage leaves
(each about 5 inches in diameter),
washed and dried

These wonderful chocolate cups form the edible containers for ice cream desserts. For the best results, melt the chocolate in batches in order to dip each leaf individually. This way the chocolate is always warm enough to spread without a lot of reheating.

By spreading the chocolate on the outside of the leaves, you'll have the imprint of the symmetrical cabbage ribs.

Line a cookie sheet with wax paper; set aside.
Arrange 3 ounces of the chocolate pieces in a circle

around the outer rim of a microwaveproof cereal bowl, leaving the center free. (Paper bowls work well for this and then can be thrown away). Heat on MEDIUM for 2 to 5 minutes or until the chocolate is just soft enough to spread, stirring after 2 minutes and then checking every 30 seconds thereafter.

When the chocolate is softened, take a small spoon, rubber spatula, or brush and spread the chocolate as evenly as possible on the outside of a cabbage leaf, being careful not to leave any holes or spread it too thinly. Place the leaf in the freezer to harden for 15 to 30 minutes.

Repeat the chocolate-melting process with the remaining chocolate and freeze on a cookie sheet when all the leaves are coated.

After the chocolate has frozen, carefully pull off the cabbage leaves and return the chocolate to a closed container for storage in the refrigerator.

NOTE: If you can't remove the cabbage leaves from the chocolate easily after removing from the freezer, allow them to sit on counter to soften slightly for 1 minute.

WEST COAST MENU

Serves 8

Avocado and Radicchio
Salad with Monterey Jack
Raclette

Coastal Chili

Green and Red Pepper
Timbales with Cilantro
Leaves

Warm Flour Tortillas

Margarita Pie

Cinnamon-Spiked Truffles

WEST COAST MENU

Avocado and Radicchio Salad with Monterey Jack Raclette

Coastal Chili

Green and Red Pepper Timbales with Cilantro Leaves

Warm Flour Tortillas

Margarita Pie

Cinnamon-Spiked Truffles

T his menu combines the variety of flavors that we remember from our trips to the West Coast. Margaritas are an excellent way to kick off the evening, with some salsa and chips, before you move on to dinner.

WINE SUGGESTION
We prefer a light beer, but Beaujolais-Villages is very nice also

PREPARATION PLAN

THE DAY BEFORE:

1. Make the pie up to the point of whipping the cream and refrigerate.
2. Make the truffles and refrigerate in a tightly sealed container.
3. Make the chili up to the point the scallops are added; refrigerate. The flavor will develop over-night and the scallops or fish are added right before serving.
4. Make the tortillas and refrigerate.
5. Make the salad dressing and refrigerate.

2 HOURS IN ADVANCE:

1. Wash the radicchio leaves.
2. Whip the cream and finish the pie.

1 HOUR BEFORE SERVING:

1. Arrange the radicchio leaves on the plates.
2. Heat the chili on HIGH for 10 to 20 minutes, or until heated through, stirring once. Add the scallops or fish for the final cooking period. It is important not to overcook the scallops for the best flavor.
3. Cook the rice.

15 MINUTES BEFORE SERVING:

1. Heat the cheese for the raclette. While the cheese is heating, cut and arrange the avocado on the lettuce plate. Drizzle the dressing over the salad.
2. Add the cheese to the salad and serve.
3. As you remove the cheese from the microwave oven, finish cooking the chili, with the shellfish added, on MEDIUM for 12 to 18 minutes.

AT THE TABLE:

1. Between the salad and chili course, and during the 5-minute standing time of the chili, form the rice timbales and reheat the tortillas on HIGH for 2 minutes.
2. Invert the rice timbales onto serving plates and garnish with cilantro leaves. Spoon the chili next to the rice. Serve the tortillas.
3. Serve the pie and truffles.

EVEN EASIER HINTS

1. Use good-quality store-bought flour tortillas.
2. Make Mango Cream (see page 148) or serve with Mango Slices and Ice Cream (see page 149) or serve fresh melon crescents with lime or lemon sherbet for dessert.
3. Don't form the rice into timbales, just spoon it onto the plates.

AVOCADO AND RADICCHIO SALAD WITH MONTEREY JACK RACLETTE

Serves: 8

Cooking time: 3 to 4 minutes

8 ounces Monterey Jack cheese, cut into slices about 2 inches square and ¼ inch thick
2 heads radicchio or red-tipped lettuce, washed and broken into leaves
4 small ripe avocados
¾ cup olive oil
3 tablespoons lemon juice
2 tablespoons Dijon mustard
½ teaspoon salt
¼ teaspoon freshly ground black pepper

Heating the cheese on the MEDIUM *power setting is important for even softening.*

Place the cheese slices in a circle on a 12-inch microwaveproof plate leaving a ½-inch space between each piece. Place in the microwave oven and cook on MEDIUM for 3 to 4 minutes until the color becomes light but the cheese is not runny, rotating plate one-half turn after 1½ minutes.

Meanwhile, arrange the radicchio leaves in a circle on each salad plate. Peel and pit the avocados, and cut them into ¼-inch slices. Divide the avocado slices among the plates and arrange them in a circle over the radicchio.

In a small bowl, combine the oil, lemon juice, mustard, salt, and pepper. Drizzle the dressing over the avocado and radicchio.

Using a spatula place a warm piece of cheese in the center of each salad and serve immediately.

COASTAL CHILI

Serves: 8

Cooking time: 22 to 32 minutes

This is an honest-to-goodness chili, but it is made with scallops rather than ground beef, to lighten it and add an exciting twist. To make ahead, just cook up to the point the scallops are added, and then refrigerate until 1 hour before serving.

In a 3-quart microwaveproof casserole, combine the oil, garlic, onion, chili, cumin, oregano, cinnamon, salt, cayenne, and black pepper. Cover with wax paper and cook on HIGH for 2 to 4 minutes or until the onion is tender-crisp. Add the remaining ingredients except the scallops. Cover again and cook on HIGH for 8 to 10 minutes or until the mixture is boiling; stir well.

Place the scallops around the outer rim of the casserole. Cover again with wax paper and cook on MEDIUM for 12 to 18 minutes, or until the scallops test done; stir to mix well. Let stand, covered, for 5 minutes before serving. Serve with rice and a dollop of sour cream.

NOTE: You may substitute any firm-fleshed fish such as monkfish, shark, or skate (cut into ½-inch pieces) for the scallops; or combine scallops and peeled, uncooked shrimps.

2 tablespoons oil
2 garlic cloves, minced
1 large onion, chopped
2 tablespoons chili powder
2 teaspoons cumin seed or ½ teaspoon ground
1 teaspoon dried oregano
1 teaspoon cinnamon
½ teaspoon salt
½ teaspoon cayenne pepper
½ teaspoon freshly ground black pepper
4 cups peeled, chopped fresh tomatoes or 2 (16-ounce) cans stewed tomatoes, drained
4 cups cooked red kidney or black beans and 1 cup cooking liquid or 2 (16-ounce) cans kidney beans, undrained
2 medium-size green peppers, seeded and coarsely chopped
2 pounds bay scallops or sea scallops, cut into ½-inch pieces
Sour cream

COOKING DRIED KIDNEY BEANS

Makes: 4 cups cooked beans plus 1 cup cooking liquid

Cooking time: 45 to 52 minutes

3 cups presoaked dried kidney or black beans
3 cups water

In a 3-quart casserole with lid combine beans and water. Cover tightly and cook on HIGH for 10 to 12 minutes, or until boiling; stir. Cover again and cook on MEDIUM for 35 to 40 minutes, or until beans are tender, stirring after 15 minutes. Let stand, covered, for 5 minutes.

SPEED SOAKING OF KIDNEY BEANS

Place 1½ cups of dried kidney beans plus 3 cups of water in a 3-quart casserole. Cover tightly. Cook on HIGH for 8 to 10 minutes to boil; stir. Then cook on MEDIUM 2 minutes. Let stand covered for 1 hour. Drain beans and cook following the above instructions. Use the drained liquid as part of the cooking liquid. Makes 3 cups presoaked beans.

GREEN AND RED PEPPER TIMBALES WITH CILANTRO LEAVES

Serves: 8

Cooking time: 19 to 24 minutes

3½ cups water
½ teaspoon salt
2 cups raw long-grain or converted rice
2 bell peppers (one red and one green),
    stems removed, seeded, and cut into
    ¼-inch cubes
Cilantro leaves or parsley, for garnish

Combine the water and salt in a 4-quart microwave-proof casserole. Stir in the rice. Cover tightly and cook on HIGH for 7 to 10 minutes or until boiling. Cook on MEDIUM for 12 to 14 minutes or until almost all the liquid has been absorbed. Stir in the peppers. Cover and let stand for 5 minutes.

To make the timbales, right before serving, spoon one eighth of the warm rice into each of eight 5- or 6-ounce custard cups or ramekins. (If the rice needs reheating at this point, cover tightly and cook on HIGH for 1 to 6 minutes, stirring every minute to ensure even heating. With a spoon, press the rice down firmly to shape, then invert onto eight serving plates.

Garnish with cilantro leaves or parsley.

NOTE: To make 4 servings, cut the ingredients in half and combine them in a 2-quart microwaveproof casserole. Cook on HIGH for 4 to 7 minutes, then on MEDIUM for 8 to 10 minutes.

WARM FLOUR TORTILLAS

Makes: 12 tortillas

Cooking time: 6 to 8 minutes

2 cups all-purpose flour
½ teaspoon salt
¼ cup vegetable shortening
½ cup warm water

In a pinch we have purchased flour tortillas, but they are never as good as these. They can be leisurely cooked a day in advance and then reheated in a tea towel, right in a wicker basket (no metal staples in the basket, please, or you'll have arcing in the oven).

We find that a food processor quickens the preparation, without eliminating the therapeutic value of rolling and stretching the dough. If you do not have a food processor, mixing with a pastry cutter or fork is possible but not nearly as easy. We give the recipe for 12 because that is what our food processor handles best; for a crowd, you may need to make two batches.

Combine the flour and salt in the bowl of a food processor and pulse, or turn on and off quickly, to mix the flour and salt. Add the shortening. Pulse again, just until the shortening is evenly mixed into the flour (five or six times). Pour the water into the feed tube and pulse until the mixture just forms a ball.

Divide the dough into 12 egg-sized balls by taking some of the dough in your hand, making a fist, and squeezing a ball out between your thumb and index finger. Lightly grease your hands with shortening, and roll each ball of dough between your hands to lightly coat it. Place the balls on the counter or a cookie sheet and cover them with a clean tea towel to rest for 15 to 30 minutes.

With a rolling pin, roll each ball into a thin circle 7 to 8 inches in diameter on a lightly floured board. Pull or gently stretch them slightly if necessary. Cook them on a hot, ungreased griddle until brown speckles appear on the undersides. Air bubbles will form on top during baking; just press these down lightly with a metal spatula to flatten them. Flip the tortillas over and cook them on the other side for about 30 seconds. Place the finished tortillas between the folds of a tea towel.

To reheat, wrap the tortillas in a tea towel and heat on HIGH for 1 to 2 minutes.

NOTE: To store for more than 2 hours, place the cooked tortillas in a plastic bag in the refrigerator. Before heating, remove from the plastic bag and wrap 6 at a time in a dampened paper towel. Heat on HIGH for 1 minute. Follow this heating procedure for store-bought tortillas, too.

CINNAMON *Cinnamon can refer to any one of several* Cinnamomum *species from Vietnam, Indonesia, or Sri Lanka. It is the bark of the* Cassia *evergreens grown in Southeast Asia that we know in this country as cinnamon (the type grown in Sri Lanka is much milder and not sold here). Harvesting commences during the rainy season when the moist bark is most manageable for removal. The inner bark is stripped from the trees and rolled into the long, slender quills that we call cinnamon sticks.* ❰ *In antiquity, cinnamon serviced the religious world in incense and anointing oils. Cinnamon has wide appeal in fruit desserts, baked goods, and many sweets. It adds dimension to Mexican chilies and winter squash, too.*

MARGARITA PIE

Serves: 8

Cooking time: 5 to 9 minutes

CRUMB CRUST:

6 tablespoons unsalted butter

1½ cups finely ground zweiback crumbs

2 tablespoons sugar

PIE FILLING:

1 cup sugar

3 tablespoons cornstarch

¼ cup unsalted butter

2 teaspoons grated lime or lemon rind

½ cup freshly squeezed lime juice

½ cup half-and-half

¼ cup tequila

1 tablespoon Triple-Sec

1 cup plain yogurt

1 cup heavy cream

2 tablespoons confectioners' sugar

2 whole limes, very thinly sliced, for garnish

Salt

If you have trouble finding zweiback cookies, check the baby food section of your grocery store.

To make the crust, place the butter in a 9-inch glass pie plate. Melt on HIGH for 1 to 2 minutes. Stir in the crumbs and sugar. Press the mixture against the sides and bottom of the dish to form an even crust. Cook on HIGH for 1½ to 2 minutes or until set.

To make the pie filling, in a 2-quart microwaveproof casserole, combine the sugar, cornstarch, butter, grated rind, lime juice, and half-and-half. Cook on HIGH for 2 minutes; stir well. Continue to cook on HIGH for 1 to 3 minutes or until thickened. Beat the mixture with an electric beater until smooth for 1 to 2 minutes. Beat in the tequila and Triple-Sec. Place the mixture in the refrigerator to cool for about 1 hour, or speed-cool in the freezer for 20 minutes. Fold in the yogurt and pour into the prepared pie shell. Smooth out the top evenly with a knife.

Whip the heavy cream and sweeten it with the confectioners' sugar. Spoon the whipped cream on top of the pie. Dip one half of each of the lime slices into the salt and insert the unsalted sides into the whipped cream around the outer rim of the pie, angling the slices toward the outside. Chill at least 1 hour until serving time.

CINNAMON-SPIKED TRUFFLES

Makes: 24 truffles

Cooking time: About 3 minutes

6 ounces semisweet chocolate pieces
3 tablespoons unsalted butter
2 large egg yolks
2 tablespoons rum
¼ cup unsweetened cocoa powder
1 teaspoon cinnamon
2 tablespoons sifted confectioners' sugar

Place the chocolate pieces in a circle in a microwave-proof cereal bowl, leaving the center open. Cook on MEDIUM for 2 minutes; stir. Cook on MEDIUM for 1 to 1½ minutes more, until the chocolate is just melted, stirring every 30 seconds.

Soften the butter to room temperature by heating it on DEFROST for 10 seconds.

In a medium mixing bowl, combine the butter, egg yolks, and rum. Add the melted chocolate and beat with a mixer until well blended, about 2 minutes. Chill for 30 minutes or until the mixture can be rolled into a ball.

Sift the cocoa, cinnamon, and confectioners' sugar together into a small bowl. Line a cookie sheet with wax paper. Take 1 tablespoon of the chilled chocolate mixture and roll it into a ball. Roll it in the cocoa mixture and place it on the cookie sheet. Repeat this process with the rest of the mixture. Chill until firm, then store in a tightly sealed container in the refrigerator or freezer.

Serve with dessert, as a cake garnish, or with coffee.

Variations:

SAMBUCA-ESPRESSO TRUFFLES: Substitute Sambuca for the rum. Wrap each tablespoon of the chilled chocolate mixture around an espresso coffee bean. Great with espresso coffee!

IRISH WHISKEY TRUFFLES: Substitute Irish Whiskey for the rum. Wrap each tablespoon of the chilled chocolate mixture around a coffee bean. Add 1 teaspoon instant espresso powder to the cocoa and sugar mixture before rolling the truffles.

VEAL DAUBE IS A CHILLY SPRING NIGHT'S DINING

Serves 8

Baked Brie with Figs and
Raspberry Vinegar

Chinos Three-Pepper
Mélange on Pastry
Diamonds

Veal Daube with Wild and
Domestic Mushrooms

Buttered Egg Noodles with
Poppy Seeds

Crusty Bread

Warm Mixed-Green Salad
with Sun-Dried Tomatoes

Piña Colada Ice Cream
Scoops

Hot Fudge Sauce

VEAL DAUBE IS A CHILLY SPRING NIGHT'S DINING

This menu is the meeting of two cultures: Eastern Europe, with its delicious saucy veal and mushroom daube, and California, with the touches of figs, Raspberry Vinegar, tri-color bell peppers, and piña colada dessert. The unlikely marriage is at once warming to the soul and exciting to the eye and palate. Enjoy it by the fire while winter breathes its last gasp. The cascades of basil-scented peppers on thin, flaky pastry make for a sensational first course. We call them pastry diamonds, but they can be tailor-made to any shape suitable to your appetizer plates. Chinos, by the way, is the famous farm in Southern California that supplies many of the great restaurants there with produce.

PREPARATION PLAN

THE DAY BEFORE:
1. Prepare the daube up to the point the crème fraîche is added; refrigerate.
2. Prepare the dough for the pastry diamonds and refrigerate.
3. Prepare the pepper mélange, if desired, and refrigerate, or make it 2 hours before serving time.
4. Toast the coconut, prepare and freeze the ice cream balls, and slice the pineapple for the dessert.

1½ HOURS BEFORE SERVING:
1. Remove the pepper mélange from the refrigerator to bring to room temperature.
2. Roll out and cook the pastry diamonds.
3. Prepare the lettuce, tomatoes, and salad dressing, but do not combine.
4. Slice the mushrooms for the daube and wash the enoki mushrooms.

½ HOUR BEFORE SERVING:
1. Remove the daube from the refrigerator and heat on MEDIUM for 15 to 20 minutes or until hot. Continue to follow the recipe, adding the crème fraîche. Cook the mushrooms.
2. Meanwhile, chop the figs for the Brie.
3. Heat the pepper mélange, if it needs it, to bring to room temperature.
4. Boil the water for the noodles on top of the stove and cook them, keeping them warm over a pot of hot water. Set out a bowl to toss the noodles in, and measure out the poppy seeds.

15 MINUTES BEFORE SERVING:
Heat the Brie.

AT THE TABLE:
1. Serve Brie, follow with the pepper mélange and pastry diamond course. Meanwhile, reheat the daube, if necessary.
2. Remove the pepper mélange and pastry diamond course from the table; heat the salad dressing and toss with the salad. Toss the noodles with the poppy seeds and serve on the plates with the daube. Don't forget the bread.
3. Remove the veal daube course from the table; arrange and serve the dessert.

EVEN EASIER HINTS
1. Substitute Coconut-Cluster Banana Split (see page 48) for the Piña Colada Ice Cream Scoops.
2. An alternative to the egg noodles is the Molded Sage Polenta (see page 46), which can be made and molded before reheating the daube, starting 45 minutes before serving time. Reheat at the last minute.

BAKED BRIE WITH FIGS AND RASPBERRY VINEGAR

Serves: 8 to 10

Cooking time: 3 to 5 minutes

½ to 1 pound whole ripe Brie cheese
3 to 4 dried figs, finely chopped (¼ to ⅓ cup)
¼ cup Raspberry Vinegar (recipe follows) or store-bought
Fresh raspberries, tarragon, or dill, for garnish
Water crackers

This is a quick and delicious way to serve Brie, so that it is just warm enough to easily spread on crackers. We think you'll find that even those who don't love Brie—or who think they don't—are enticed by this combination of flavors.

Cut the Brie horizontally into halves. Place the halves skin side down on a microwaveproof serving platter. Sprinkle the top evenly with the chopped figs. Drizzle the vinegar over the top. Cook the cheese on MEDIUM for 3 to 5 minutes or until the cheese is just softened but not runny.

Garnish on the side with fresh raspberries or herbs. Serve with crackers.

RASPBERRY VINEGAR

Makes: ¼ to ⅓ cup

Cooking time: 2 minutes

1 (10-ounce) package frozen raspberries
2 tablespoons red wine vinegar

Remove the raspberries from their packaging if it is metal (leave in a paper container) and place in a microwaveproof bowl. Heat on DEFROST for 2 minutes. Let stand 5 minutes.

Drain the raspberry juice into a 1-cup glass measure or a small bowl—you should get about ¼ cup—and reserve the raspberries for another use. Add the vinegar to the juice and stir.

CHINOS THREE-PEPPER MÉLANGE ON PASTRY DIAMONDS

Serves: 8

Cooking time: 15 to 19 minutes

To make the pastry, combine the flour and cheese in a food processor or mixing bowl and mix well. With the food processor blade or a pastry blender, cut in the butter until the particles are pea size. Blend in the egg. Form the dough into a ball, being careful not to overwork the dough, or it will become tough. Flatten the dough into a square about ½ inch thick. Wrap in plastic wrap and chill for at least 1 hour or overnight.

To make the pepper mélange, combine the oil, garlic, onions, and peppers in a 2-quart microwaveproof casserole. Cook on HIGH for 8 minutes or until the vegetables are tender, stirring after 4 minutes. Stir in the basil, oregano, and thyme. Cover again and cook on HIGH for 1 minute. Set aside. It is best to serve the pepper mélange slightly warm or at room temperature.

Remove the pastry dough from the refrigerator and roll out into an 11½-inch square that is approximately ⅛ inch thick. Using a pastry wheel (for a more decorative pastry) or knife, cut the pastry into 8 diamonds to fit your serving plates.

Line the microwave oven (bottom shelf) with a double thickness of wax paper. Place 4 pastries at a time on the wax paper. Cook, uncovered, on HIGH for 3 to 5 minutes or until the pastries appear opaque and dry, repositioning them if necessary. Slide onto a cooling rack, and cook the remaining pastries.

To serve, place a pastry on each serving plate and spoon some pepper mélange on top of each.

NOTE: If you have made the pepper mélange in advance and refrigerated it, take the chill off by heating it, covered, on HIGH for 2 to 5 minutes or until slightly warm, stirring once.

PASTRY:
1 cup all-purpose flour
2 tablespoons grated Parmesan cheese
5 tablespoons unsalted butter
1 egg, beaten

PEPPER MÉLANGE:
2 tablespoons olive oil
2 garlic cloves, minced
2 cups thinly sliced onions
3 medium-size bell peppers (red, green, and yellow), seeded and cut into ¼-inch cubes
½ cup chopped fresh basil
¼ teaspoon dried oregano
¼ teaspoon dried thyme

VEAL DAUBE WITH WILD AND DOMESTIC MUSHROOMS

Serves: 8

Cooking time: 1 hour and 10 minutes to 1 hour and 40 minutes

1 ounce dried morel mushrooms

2 tablespoons unsalted butter

2 garlic cloves, minced

1 cup chopped onions

3½ pounds veal shoulder, cut into 1-inch cubes

3 tablespoons all-purpose flour

1 tablespoon chopped fresh tarragon or 1 teaspoon dried

1 tablespoon tomato paste

1¾ cups chicken broth

½ cup medium-dry red wine (Beaujolais is nice)

2 tablespoons brandy (optional)

2 tablespoons lemon juice

½ teaspoon salt

¼ teaspoon freshly ground black pepper

¼ cup crème fraîche, sour cream, or heavy cream

1 pound mushrooms, cut into ¼-inch slices

1 (2-ounce) package enoki mushrooms, trimmed at the base (optional)

Sprigs of fresh tarragon, for garnish

A daube, or fancy stew, is wonderful for entertaining because it can be prepared in advance and in fact tastes better when it has had a chance to develop its flavors overnight. This daube showcases mushrooms—the rich, woodsy flavor of dried morels, the succulence of sautéed domestic mushrooms, and the texture and shape of raw tiny white enoki mushrooms. You'll find this an extremely satisfying and comforting main course.

Soak the morels in warm water in a small bowl until soft, about 15 minutes. Rinse, drain, and chop.

Meanwhile, in a 3-quart microwaveproof casserole, combine the butter, garlic, and onions. Cook on HIGH for 3 to 5 minutes or until tender. In a large plastic bag or bowl, toss the veal cubes with the flour to coat well.

Add the veal to the onions. Cover tightly and cook on HIGH for 16 to 18 minutes or until little or no pink color remains, stirring often after 8 minutes. Stir in the chopped morels, the tarragon, tomato paste, broth, wine, brandy, lemon juice, salt, and pepper. Cover again and cook on HIGH for 8 to 12 minutes or until boiling; stir. Cover again and cook on MEDIUM for 40 to 60 minutes or until the meat is tender, stirring twice.

Stir in the crème fraîche. Cover and let stand for 10 minutes.

Meanwhile, place the sliced mushrooms in a 1-quart microwaveproof casserole. Cook, uncovered, on HIGH for 3 to 6 minutes, stirring after 2 minutes. Stir into the veal mixture. Serve over the Buttered Egg Noodles with

44

Poppy Seeds on individual plates, sprinkling the top of each serving with enoki mushrooms, if desired. Garnish with tarragon.

NOTE: When made ahead and refrigerated, the daube can be heated on MEDIUM 15 to 20 minutes or until hot; stir twice during heating time. Stir in the crème fraîche; cover and let stand for 10 minutes.

BUTTERED EGG NOODLES WITH POPPY SEEDS

Serves: 8

Cooking time: 20 minutes

1 (16-ounce) package egg noodles
Salt
⅓ cup unsalted butter
¼ cup poppy seeds

Boil a large quantity of water on top of the stove to cook the noodles. Salt the water slightly and cook the noodles according to package directions until tender.

Drain the noodles in a colander, reserving about half of the boiling water and returning it to the cooking pot. Cover it to keep warm.

Meanwhile, place the butter in a 1-cup glass measure and melt on HIGH in the microwave oven for 30 to 45 seconds; then toss with the noodles in a bowl. Transfer the buttered noodles back to the colander, set over the hot water, and cover until serving time.

Right before serving, return the noodles to the bowl and toss with the poppy seeds.

MOLDED SAGE POLENTA

Serves: 8

Cooking time: 13 to 18 minutes

½ cup unsalted butter
1 medium-size onion, finely chopped
1½ cups coarse yellow cornmeal
½ teaspoon salt
5 cups water
¾ cup grated Parmesan cheese
8 fresh sage leaves

In a 3-quart microwaveproof casserole, combine the butter and onion. Cook on HIGH for 2 to 4 minutes or until the onion is tender. Stir in the cornmeal, mixing well. Stir in the water and salt slowly. Cover tightly and cook on HIGH for 6 minutes. Stir to mix well. Cover again and cook on HIGH for 5 to 8 minutes, until all the water is absorbed, stirring once again. Stir in the cheese.

Place 1 sage leaf, right side down, in the bottom of eight individual 5- to 6-ounce ramekins or custard cups. Spoon the cooked polenta into each ramekin. Let stand for 10 minutes or until serving time. Unmold onto individual serving plates or one large serving platter.

NOTE: To reheat room-temperature polenta, cover the ramekins with plastic wrap and heat on MEDIUM for 3 to 8 minutes, until warm to the touch.

MICROWAVE "SUN-DRIED" TOMATOES

Makes: ¼ cup

Cooking time: 45 to 50 minutes

4 plum tomatoes (½ pound), cut in half lengthwise
⅛ teaspoon salt
Olive oil

In Mastering Microwave Cookery, *we compared sunlight to microwave energy and so we decided to carry this idea a little bit further and use it to dry tomatoes.*

The process still takes a bit of time, but it certainly is more efficient than drying the tomatoes a few days in the sun. The results are tomatoes with a concentrated, rich, pungent flavor that will do much for a pasta sauce.

Line a 12-inch microwaveproof plate with paper towels and place the tomatoes on top, with space in between the thinner ends toward the inside.

Cook on DEFROST for 20 minutes. Rotate the plate a half-turn and continue to cook on DEFROST for 20 minutes more. Discard the paper towel and replace with another piece. Cook on DEFROST for 5 to 10 minutes more or until the tomatoes are dried but no burn spots appear.

Season with the salt and place in a small dish. Cover with olive oil. Let stand overnight or for a few days.

WARM MIXED-GREEN SALAD WITH SUN-DRIED TOMATOES

Combine the lettuce and dried tomatoes in a salad bowl. Toss to mix. Let stand at room temperature.

In a 1-cup glass measure, combine the oils, vinegar, and lemon juice. Heat on HIGH for 2 to 3 minutes or until warm. Pour over the lettuce and tomatoes. Toss and serve.

Serves: 8

Cooking time: 2 to 3 minutes

8 cups washed, torn lettuce leaves (red-tipped, Bibb, Boston, and/or romaine, mixed)
¼ cup sliced sun-dried tomatoes, packed in olive oil
¼ cup vegetable oil
2 tablespoons olive oil
1 tablespoon sesame oil
⅓ cup red wine or sherry vinegar
1 tablespoon lemon juice

47

PIÑA COLADA ICE CREAM SCOOPS

Serves: 8

Cooking time: 10 to 15 minutes

1½ cups packaged grated coconut,
    sweetened
1 quart French vanilla ice cream
1 whole ripe pineapple, peeled, cored, and
    sliced into 8 rings
8 to 16 green pineapple leaves

Place ½ cup of the coconut on a cookie sheet. Toast in the conventional oven at 350°F until lightly browned, about 10 to 15 minutes, stirring occasionally. Set aside to cool and then store in a plastic container.

Meanwhile, place the remaining 1 cup coconut on a piece of wax paper. Scoop out 8 balls of ice cream; roll each in the untoasted coconut and then place them on a cookie sheet to freeze.

To serve, place a pineapple slice on each dessert plate and garnish each with 1 or 2 pineapple leaves. Top the center of the pineapple with one of the prepared scoops of ice cream. Sprinkle the top of each with toasted coconut before serving.

Variation:

COCONUT-CLUSTER BANANA SPLIT: Reduce the amount of coconut to just the ½ cup toasted coconut. Substitute 4 bananas for the pineapple.

To serve, peel and cut each banana in half crosswise. Cut each half in half again lengthwise and place each open-face on eight dessert plates. Top with a scoop of ice cream and spoon on some Hot Fudge Sauce (recipe follows). Sprinkle with toasted coconut.

HOT FUDGE SAUCE

In a 4-cup glass measure, combine the chocolate, half-and-half, and corn syrup. Cook on HIGH for 2 minutes; stir. Cook on HIGH for 1 to 3 minutes more or until smooth, stirring each minute. Stir in the vanilla. Serve warm over ice cream.

Makes: 1½ cups

Cooking time: 3 to 5 minutes

6 ounces semisweet chocolate pieces
½ cup half-and-half
¼ cup light corn syrup
1 teaspoon vanilla extract

CRISP DUCK MENU

Serves 4

Marinated Vegetables with Pine Nuts Served on a Bed of Arugula

Crusty French Bread

Crisp Duck with Balsamic-Cranberry Sauce

Rice Pilaf with Asparagus

Glistening Chocolate-Pecan Cake with Fresh Raspberry Sauce
or
Peppered Pink Pears with Nutmeg Cream

CRISP DUCK MENU

T his is one of our favorite menus and is sure to please anyone who likes duck. We like to serve this at an intimate New Year's gathering with lots of sparkling Champagne.

WINE SUGGESTION
Zinfandel, red Rhône, or
Champagne for New Year's

PREPARATION PLAN

THE DAY BEFORE OR UP TO 3 HOURS BEFORE SERVING:

1. Marinate the vegetables.
2. Make and glaze the cake or prepare the pears and refrigerate if not using that day.
3. Make the raspberry sauce and refrigerate if not using that day.
4. Make the balsamic-cranberry sauce for the duck and refrigerate if not using that day.
5. Truss the duck for cooking.

1½ HOURS BEFORE SERVING:

1. Prepare the rice pilaf.
2. While the pilaf is cooking, wash the arugula.
3. Arrange the vegetables on individual plates.
4. Allow the rice to stand covered, and cook the duck.
5. When the duck is removed from the conventional oven, let it stand, and serve the vegetables and bread course.

AT THE TABLE:

1. Remove the vegetable plates and cut up the duck.
2. Meanwhile, reheat the rice and balsamic-cranberry sauce, if necessary. The sauce will take 2 to 3 minutes on HIGH.
3. Arrange the plates with the duck and rice, and serve.
4. For dessert, cut the cake and heat the raspberry sauce, if desired, or serve the Peppered Pink Pears with Nutmeg Cream.

OLIVE OIL *Olive oil is a monosaturated oil that nutritionists now consider to be beneficial because it lowers the body's harmful blood cholesterol but leaves the beneficial cholesterol intact. ❧ Good extra-virgin olive oil is very fragrant and fruity and doesn't have to cost an arm and a leg. According to United States standards, "virgin oil" means an unrefined oil from the first pressing. Look for a deep green-golden color, which means that it will be fuller in flavor. Two different styles are evident in the milder French Louis de Regis or an Italian Badia a Coltibuono, with an almost peppery aftertaste. ❧ Olive oil should be consumed rather quickly or, if purchased in large containers, it should be decanted into smaller bottles for less exposure to the air since air spoils its flavor. It is best to store these bottles in the dark, or to pour the oil into cans that protect it from the light.*

MARINATED VEGETABLES WITH PINE NUTS SERVED ON A BED OF ARUGULA

Serves: 4

Cooking time: 5 minutes

MARINADE:

3 tablespoons olive oil

1 tablespoon balsamic vinegar

1 teaspoon Dijon mustard

VEGETABLES:

12 ounces mushrooms, quartered

1 pound green snap beans

1 bunch arugula, washed, dried, and separated

2 pimientos, cut into ¼-inch strips

¼ cup toasted pine nuts

Combine the marinade ingredients in a 2-quart microwaveproof casserole. Add the mushrooms. Cook, uncovered, on HIGH for 2 minutes, stirring once. Reserving the marinade, transfer the mushrooms with a slotted spoon into a bowl.

Add the green beans to the marinade. Cover tightly and cook on HIGH for 3 minutes or until the beans are tender-crisp, stirring once halfway through the cooking. Spoon into the bowl next to mushrooms and pour the remaining marinade over the beans. Cover and chill for at least 1 hour.

To serve, arrange the arugula leaves in spoke fashion on each plate. Place the green beans on top of the arugula leaves, without covering the tips of the leaves. Spoon the mushrooms over the beans. Arrange the pimiento strips on top of the mushrooms. Sprinkle each plate with 1 tablespoon of the pine nuts and drizzle with the marinade.

RICE PILAF WITH ASPARAGUS

Serves: 4

Cooking time: 13 to 19 minutes

¼ cup unsalted butter
1 garlic clove, minced
1 medium-size onion, finely chopped
1 cup long-grain or converted rice
1¾ cups chicken broth
1 pound asparagus, trimmed, peeled, and
    cut into 1-inch pieces
2 tablespoons chopped fresh parsley

The rice will stay warm for up to an hour, but if you need to reheat before serving or preparing the timbales, cover tightly and heat on HIGH for 1 to 6 minutes, depending on the starting temperature of the rice, stirring every minute.

In a 3-quart microwaveproof casserole, combine the butter, garlic, and onion. Cook on HIGH for 2 to 3 minutes or until the onion is tender but not brown.

Stir in the rice, coating every grain. Stir in the broth. Cover tightly and cook on HIGH for 4 to 6 minutes or until boiling. Reduce the power to MEDIUM and cook for 5 minutes. Stir in the asparagus. Continue to cook on MEDIUM for 2 to 5 minutes or until most of the liquid has been absorbed and the rice is tender. Stir in the parsley. Cover again and let stand for 5 minutes.

To serve, either spoon the warm rice onto each serving plate, or prepare timbales. Right before serving, spoon the warm rice into six 5- to 6-ounce ramekins or custard cups. Press the rice firmly into the cups and invert onto the serving plates.

NOTE: Since we often serve this in the winter, we substitute 1 cup finely grated carrots for the asparagus.

CRISP DUCK WITH BALSAMIC-CRANBERRY SAUCE

Serves: 4 (with 2 cups sauce)

Cooking time: 48 to 55 minutes

1 (5-pound) duck

BALSAMIC-CRANBERRY SAUCE:
½ pound fresh or unsweetened frozen
    cranberries
7 tablespoons sugar
2 tablespoons orange-flavored liqueur
¼ cup balsamic vinegar
1 cup Duck Giblet Stock (recipe follows)
    or ½ cup, each, chicken and beef
    broth
1 teaspoon chopped fresh ginger
Dash cayenne pepper

Remove the fat from the body cavity and neck of the duck. Remove the giblets and reserve if planning to make the giblet stock. Tie the legs together with string and crisscross over the back to tie the wings to the body. Prick the skin to allow the fat to ooze out. Place the duck, breast side down, on a microwaveproof roasting rack in a 2-quart rectangular glass dish. Cook in the microwave oven on HIGH for 15 minutes. Remove from the microwave oven and pour off the fat. Turn the duck to breast side up. Return to the microwave oven and cook on HIGH for 10 minutes or until the juices run clear. Meanwhile, preheat the conventional oven to 500°F.

After the duck has cooked in the microwave oven, pour off the fat. Place the duck in the conventional oven, breast side down, on a metal roasting rack in the same 2-quart dish to brown, about 5 minutes. Turn the duck over and continue browning for 5 minutes more. Remove and let stand, tented with foil, for 5 to 10 minutes.

Meanwhile, prepare the Balsamic-Cranberry Sauce. In a 1½-quart microwaveproof casserole, combine the cranberries, 4 tablespoons of the sugar, and the liqueur. Cover with wax paper and cook in the microwave oven on HIGH for 2 to 5 minutes or until the berries have popped, stirring after 2 minutes. Remove and set aside.

In a 1-quart microwaveproof casserole, combine the vinegar and the remaining 3 tablespoons sugar. Cook, uncovered, in the microwave oven on HIGH for 3 minutes; stir. Cook on HIGH for 1 to 2 minutes more or until the mixture begins to thicken and coat a spoon (be careful not to let it burn). Stir the stock and ginger slowly into the syrup. Add the cranberry mixture and cayenne. Cook on HIGH for 2 to 4 minutes or until boiling; stir. Cook on HIGH for 5 minutes more to develop the flavor.

NOTE: If legs and wings of duck start to overcook in microwave oven, cover these sections with aluminum foil to prevent further cooking.

Variations:

GRILLED DUCK: To grill the duck instead of baking it in the conventional oven, cut it into quarters before cooking in the microwave oven. Follow the same microwave cooking instructions, and meanwhile preheat the grill. Grill the duck for 5 minutes on each side, skin side down first, while watching closely to prevent burning.

CRISP ROAST DUCK WITH FRESH FIG SAUCE: Eliminate the Balsamic-Cranberry Sauce and while the duck is cooking in the oven or while it is standing, trim 1 pound fresh figs plus 4 whole fresh figs for garnish. Coarsely chop the pound of figs and combine, in a 2-quart microwaveproof casserole, with ¼ cup port wine, 3 tablespoons fresh lime juice, 2 tablespoons brown sugar, and 1 tablespoon unsalted butter. Cover with wax paper and cook in the microwave oven on HIGH for 7 to 8 minutes, stirring after 4 minutes, until the figs are cooked and the flavors developed. Serve at room temperature.

To serve, place one quarter of the duck on each plate and spoon ¼ cup sauce next to it. Garnish with a whole fresh fig that has been cut in half lengthwise. Spoon the remaining sauce into a serving bowl and pass at the table.

BALSAMIC VINEGAR

Balsamic vinegar is not just any wine vinegar. During the cooking of the grapes, the fruit's sugar caramelizes, creating a unique sable color and deep, rich flavor. The liquid is then aged in wooden barrels, where it mellows and becomes more concentrated. ❡ In Italy, when aceto balsamico *is aged long enough and well enough, it is even served as an after-dinner liqueur. The product sold in this country is more often added in dashes to sauces, salads, and marinades. In these instances, it will add a flurry of vibrant flavor and may eliminate the need for salt.*

DUCK GIBLET STOCK

Makes: 1 cup

Cooking time: 35 to 38 minutes

Giblets from 1 (5-pound) duck
2 cups beef broth
1 onion, quartered
1 celery rib, coarsely chopped
1 carrot, sliced

Combine all the ingredients in a 4-cup glass measure. Cover tightly and cook on HIGH for 5 to 8 minutes or until boiling; then cook on MEDIUM for 30 minutes or until the broth is reduced to 1 cup, stirring twice (it will measure 2 cups with the giblets and vegetables). Strain the stock and discard the giblets and vegetables.

GLISTENING CHOCOLATE-PECAN CAKE WITH FRESH RASPBERRY SAUCE

Serves: 6 to 8

Cooking time: 17 to 23 minutes

Vegetable shortening, for greasing mold
½ cup unsalted butter, cut into 4 pieces
½ cup sugar
2 large eggs
½ cup raspberry preserves
1 cup coarsely chopped pecans
1 cup fine dry bread crumbs
3 tablespoons unsweetened cocoa
1 teaspoon baking powder

This is a nice dessert to serve when you want to move from the dining room table to more comfortable surroundings. It can easily be eaten with a fork only, resting on your lap.

Cut two circles of wax paper to fit the bottom inside of an 8½-inch round microwaveproof cake dish. Put three small dabs of shortening on the inside bottom of the dish and place the wax paper circles on top. Set aside.

In a large mixing bowl, combine the butter and sugar and beat with a mixer until creamy. Add the eggs and preserves; beat well.

In a separate bowl, combine the pecans, bread

crumbs, cocoa, and baking powder. Add to the egg mixture. Add the Framboise and vanilla; stir well to blend. (To mix in food processor: Add the sugar, pecans, bread crumbs, cocoa, and baking powder to the processor bowl. Pulse 3 to 4 times to combine. Add butter; pulse 3 to 4 times to blend well. Add eggs, raspberry preserves, and vanilla. Process until well blended.)

Spread the batter evenly in the prepared cake dish. Place the dish on top of a microwaveproof cereal bowl in the microwave oven. Cook on MEDIUM for 8 minutes, then on HIGH for 4 to 6 minutes or until a toothpick inserted in the center comes out clean, rotating one-quarter turn once or twice if necessary. (The top will appear slightly moist but not wet.) Let the cake stand directly on the counter for 10 minutes before turning out.

To turn out, cut around the rim of the dish with a knife to loosen the cake. Invert it onto a serving plate and firmly tap the bottom of the dish to release it; peel away the wax paper. Let the cake cool completely before covering it with the glaze. After glazing the cake, decorate it with pecan halves or fresh raspberries.

To serve, spoon a little of Fresh Raspberry Sauce onto each serving plate next to the cake.

Variation:

GLISTENING CHOCOLATE-PAPRIKA CAKE: Increase the sugar to ¾ cup. Eliminate the raspberry preserves. Add 1 tablespoon paprika and 1 tablespoon grated lemon rind to the pecan mixture. Substitute brandy for the Framboise. Follow the basic cooking and serving instructions, eliminating the pecan halves or fresh raspberry garnish and Fresh Raspberry Sauce. Decorate the cake with a ring of fresh mint.

2 tablespoons Framboise, kirsch, or orange-flavored liqueur
1 teaspoon vanilla extract
Chocolate Glaze (recipe follows)
Pecan halves or ½ pint fresh raspberries, for garnish
Fresh Raspberry Sauce (recipe follows)

DECORATING GLISTENING CHOCOLATE-PECAN CAKE

To decorate the pecan cake, garnish the top edge with truffles. Place 3 ounces semisweet chocolate pieces in a Ziplock sandwich bag, moving all the pieces to one corner but keeping in a single layer. Heat on MEDIUM for 3 minutes to melt. (Push with a finger to see if it is all very soft.) With a scissor, snip a small corner off where the chocolate is melted and draw 8 lines across the cake, first to make halves, then quarters, and then eighths, to mark out 16 pieces. Place 16 small truffles around the edge, between the lines, securing them with a dab of the melted chocolate. This method of drizzling chocolate is also effective when adding a contrast to truffles and fruit.

CHOCOLATE GLAZE

Makes: Enough to coat 1 cake layer

Cooking time: 2 to 4 minutes

¼ cup light cream or half-and-half
4 ounces semisweet chocolate pieces
1 tablespoon Framboise, kirsch, orange
  liqueur, brandy, or vanilla extract

Combine all the ingredients in a 2-cup glass measure. Cook on HIGH for 1½ minutes; stir. Cook on HIGH for 30 seconds to 2⅓ minutes more or until the chocolate is soft and spreadable, stirring every 30 seconds.

Remove from the microwave oven and beat with a spoon for 2 to 4 minutes or just until the chocolate is well blended, thickened, and smooth. Pour over the cooled cake and smooth quickly with a spatula.

FRESH RASPBERRY SAUCE

Makes: 1⅓ cup

Cooking time: 3 to 5 minutes

2 cups fresh raspberries or 1 (12-ounce)
  package frozen, unsweetened, thawed
¼ cup sugar
2 tablespoons Framboise, kirsch, or 1
  tablespoon vanilla extract

This sauce adds bright color and wonderful flavor to cakes, fresh or poached fruits, and ice cream and sherbets.

Place berries and sugar in a 4-cup glass measure and cook on HIGH for 3 to 5 minutes, until berries release their juices. Puree in a food processor or blender. Strain puree and discard seeds; stir in Framboise. Serve warm or chilled.

PEPPERED PINK PEARS WITH NUTMEG CREAM

Serves: 4

Cooking time: 12 to 14 minutes

4 medium-size firm ripe Bosc pears
1 lemon, quartered
½ cup sugar
¼ cup red wine
1 bay leaf, crushed
¼ teaspoon freshly grated nutmeg
1 teaspoon black peppercorns
½ cup crème fraîche or ½ cup whipped heavy cream sweetened with 1 tablespoon sugar
Freshly grated nutmeg

Keeping the stems intact, core the pears so that they retain their shape by cutting a cone out of the base with a grapefruit knife or other small knife. Peel the pears and rub with the cut lemon to prevent discoloration. Set the pears aside and reserve the lemon quarters.

In a 2-quart microwaveproof casserole, combine the sugar, wine, bay leaf, nutmeg, peppercorns, and lemon quarters. Cook on HIGH for 2 minutes or until the sugar is dissolved, stirring once. Place the pears on their sides in the casserole, positioning the thicker ends toward the outside. Cover tightly and cook on HIGH for 6 minutes. Baste the pears and turn them over. Cover again and cook on HIGH for 4 to 6 minutes more, until tender. Let them cool in the liquid, turning them over occasionally. Serve warm or at room temperature, or refrigerate for up to 2 days.

To serve, strain the cooking liquid and divide among four goblets. Add a poached pear to each goblet and serve with a dollop of crème fraîche or sweetened whipped cream topped with a grating of nutmeg.

BUFFET
CHILI PARTY

Serves 12 to 16

Guacamole with Bacon

Salsa Cruda with Warmed
Corn Chips

On-the-Border Ground
Beef Chili

Green Chili with Pork
Cubes
or
Green Chicken Chili

Vegetarian Chili

Flour Tortillas

Cinnamon- and Paprika-
Dusted Chocolate Ice Cream
Balls with Minted English
Cream
or
Warm Pineapple Slices with
Orange Sherbet

Buffet Chili Party

This is one of the easiest and most enjoyable ways of entertaining informally, because you will be able to relax and enjoy the party as much as your guests. ❦ All of the cooking is done the day before, so that it is just a matter of reheating the chilies on the day of the party. You can prepare two or three chilies, depending on the number of guests you invite or how many leftovers you want for yourself. Guests will serve themselves to one or more chili and garnish them as they like, with one or more of the many toppings. ❦ The quantities given in each chili recipe are based on the assumption that you will want to offer at least two and that most guests will sample small portions of each. To offer just one, increase quantities accordingly. ❦ The guacamole and salsa cruda may be served before dinner with drinks or along with the chilies at dinnertime.

PREPARATION PLAN

UP TO 3 DAYS BEFORE THE PARTY:
1. Cook the chilies and refrigerate.
2. Freeze the ice cream balls that have been coated with cinnamon.

THE DAY BEFORE OR THE MORNING OF THE PARTY:
1. Prepare the chili toppings and place them in bowls; cover and refrigerate, if necessary.
2. Prepare pineapple slices for cooking.
3. Prepare the guacamole and refrigerate.
4. Make the salsa and refrigerate.
5. Make, cook, and refrigerate the tortillas (see page 32).
6. Make the Minted English Cream for ice cream; refrigerate.

1 HOUR BEFORE SERVING:
1. Take the chilies out of the refrigerator and begin reheating them (this will take about 20 minutes each). Start with the vegetarian, then the ground beef, and finally the pork or chicken.
2. Set the table with the bowls of unrefrigerated toppings.

15 MINUTES BEFORE SERVING:
1. Set out the guacamole, salsa cruda and chips, and chilled toppings.
2. Reheat the tortillas in a cloth-lined basket on HIGH for 2 minutes.
3. Set out the heated chilies.

TO SERVE DESSERT:
After the meal has been served, heat the pineapple slices. Serve the pineapple with the sherbet or the ice cream with Minted English Cream.

EVEN EASIER HINTS
1. Substitute Lime Sherbet with Tequila (see page 73) for the dessert.
2. Purchase flour tortillas; the best-quality are homemade from a Mexican grocery store.

GUACAMOLE WITH BACON

Makes: About 4 cups

Cooking time: 6 to 10 minutes

8 slices bacon
4 ripe avocados
¼ cup fresh lime juice
2 medium-size ripe tomatoes, peeled,
    seeded, and chopped
½ cup finely minced onion
2 jalapeño or serrano chili peppers,
    seeded and finely chopped
½ teaspoon salt
¼ teaspoon freshly ground black pepper
Fresh cilantro leaves, minced, for garnish

This guacamole can be served as an appetizer with chips, or as a side chili addition. It's even good as a salad, scooped onto lettuce leaves.

Cook 4 pieces of bacon at a time by placing the bacon between paper towels on a microwave bacon rack. Cook on HIGH for 3 to 5 minutes or until crisp. Set aside. Repeat with remaining 4 pieces.

Meanwhile, halve the avocados, remove the seeds, and scoop out the pulp. With a nonaluminum fork, coarsely mash the avocado. Fold in the remaining ingredients except the cilantro. Spoon into a serving bowl and sprinkle with cilantro.

CHILIES *Peppers existed in South America first and were introduced to Europe through the discovery of the Americas. There are many varieties, but we will limit our classification to hot and mild. Generally, those with the pointier ends will be the hotter ones and the "bite" will be in the white membrane holding the seeds. ❡ The Anaheim or California pepper is usually between 4 and 6 inches long and 1½ inches in diameter and is mild, unlike the shorter hotter jalapeño and serrano peppers.*

SALSA CRUDA WITH WARMED CORN CHIPS

This raw tomato mixture makes a tasty dip for corn chips or is delicious when spooned on top of a ground beef chili.

Combine all the ingredients in the bowl of a food processor and pulse on and off 4 or 5 times until you have a coarsely chopped mixture, or coarsely chop the ingredients by hand and blend in a bowl. Serve at room temperature or chilled.

NOTE: To heat the corn chips, line a basket or ceramic bowl with a paper or cloth napkin. Place 12 ounces corn chips in the bowl. Heat on HIGH for 1 minute.

For this size crowd I usually double the recipe, making one batch at a time for best control of consistency.

Makes: About 2 cups

Cooking time: 1 minute

2 medium-size ripe tomatoes, stems removed and quartered
1 medium-size onion, peeled and quartered
2 jalapeño peppers, stems removed (seeded if a milder sauce is desired)
1 tablespoon lime juice
1 tablespoon water
1 tablespoon chopped cilantro
½ teaspoon salt

CHILI TOPPINGS

On-the-Border Ground Beef Chili

Grated Monterey Jack or Cheddar cheese

Thinly sliced green onions

Red pepper flakes

Green Chili with Pork Cubes or Green Chicken Chili

Sliced black olives

Sour cream

Lime slices

Vegetarian Chili

Sunflower seeds

Chopped fresh cilantro

Yogurt

ON-THE-BORDER GROUND BEEF CHILI

Serves: 8

Cooking time: About 1 hour

1 tablespoon vegetable oil

2 garlic cloves, minced

2 large onions, coarsely chopped

2 pounds lean ground beef

4 cups peeled and chopped fresh tomatoes
    or 2 (16-ounce) cans stewed tomatoes,
    undrained

4 cups cooked kidney or black beans with
    1 cup cooking liquid, or 2 (16-ounce)
    cans, undrained (see page 32)

2 green peppers, coarsely chopped

1 jalapeño pepper, chopped

1 (6-ounce) can tomato paste

3 to 6 tablespoons chili powder

1 tablespoon whole cumin seed or
    1 teaspoon ground

1 teaspoon dried oregano

1 teaspoon cinnamon

½ ounce unsweetened chocolate, chopped
    (about 2 tablespoons)

1 teaspoon salt

½ teaspoon freshly ground black pepper

2 tablespoons tequila

We have many ground beef chili recipes, but this one has proved to be our favorite. It was developed after a visit to the Southwest and Mexico, where we found that the cinnamon and chocolate added richness and rounded out the spicy flavor. If you have never tasted a chili made with chocolate, try this one—you'll love it.

In a 4-quart microwaveproof casserole, combine the oil, garlic, and onions. Cook on HIGH for 3 to 5 minutes or until tender-crisp. Stir in the beef, spreading it out evenly over the dish. Cook, uncovered, on HIGH for 10 to 13 minutes or until just a slight pink color remains, stirring after 5 minutes. Stir at the end of cooking. Drain the excess fat, if desired.

Stir in the remaining ingredients. Cover tightly and cook on HIGH for 10 minutes; stir. Cover again and cook on MEDIUM for 40 minutes, stirring once or twice. Let stand for 5 to 10 minutes before serving.

GREEN CHILI WITH PORK CUBES

Serve this chili with sour cream, boiled rice, or flour tortillas.

In a 4-quart microwaveproof casserole, combine the oil, garlic, and onions. Cook on HIGH for 5 to 8 minutes, stirring once until tender.

Meanwhile, in a large bowl, toss the pork cubes with the flour to coat. Stir the pork into the onion mixture. Cover tightly and cook on HIGH for 15 minutes or until no pink color remains, stirring after 8 minutes to move the less cooked pieces to the outside.

Stir in the remaining ingredients. Cover tightly and cook on HIGH for 10 to 15 minutes or until boiling; stir. Cover again and cook on MEDIUM for 50 to 70 minutes or until the meat is tender and the flavors have developed.

Serves: 8 to 10

Cooking time: 1 hour 20 minutes to 1 hour 40 minutes

1 tablespoon vegetable oil

3 garlic cloves, minced

2 large onions, coarsely chopped (1 cup)

4 pounds trimmed boneless pork, cut into 1-inch cubes

¼ cup all-purpose flour

1½ pounds mild long green chilies, chopped, or 4 (4-ounce) cans chopped green mild chilies, drained

3 cups chicken broth

3 or more serrano or jalapeño chili peppers (depending on degree of hotness desired), seeded and chopped

2 teaspoons dried marjoram

1 tablespoon whole cumin seed or ½ teaspoon ground

½ teaspoon salt (optional)

½ teaspoon freshly ground black pepper

GREEN CHICKEN CHILI

Serves: 8

Cooking time: About 25 minutes

1 tablespoon olive oil

2 garlic cloves, minced

1 large onion, coarsely chopped (½ cup)

2 pounds boneless chicken cutlets, cut
    into 1-inch cubes

¼ cup all-purpose flour

1½ pounds mild, long green chilies,
    coarsely chopped, or 4 (4-ounce) cans
    chopped green, mild chilies, drained

4 cups chicken broth or stock

2 to 4 serrano or jalapeño chili peppers,
    seeded and chopped, depending on
    taste (if you prefer "hot," leave in the
    seeds)

2 teaspoons dried oregano

2 teaspoons whole cumin seed or ½
    teaspoon ground

½ teaspoon salt (optional)

¼ teaspoon freshly ground black pepper

In a 3-quart microwaveproof casserole, combine the oil, garlic, and onion. Cook on HIGH for 4 to 6 minutes or until tender, stirring once.

Add the chicken and sprinkle evenly with the flour. Stir well to coat. Cover tightly with the lid or plastic wrap turned back slightly on one side, and cook on HIGH for 6 to 8 minutes, stirring once to move the less cooked pieces to the outside.

Stir in the remaining ingredients. Cover again and cook on HIGH for 12 to 14 minutes or until the chicken is tender, the sauce thickened, and the flavors developed, stirring once in the middle of the cooking time. Let stand, covered, for 10 minutes before serving.

VEGETARIAN CHILI

We like to serve this at a chili party or as an addition to a buffet table for our vegetarian friends. It is so tasty, and the bulgur wheat gives it such a ground beef texture, that everyone will love it.

In a 3-quart microwaveproof casserole, combine the oil, garlic, onions, green peppers, and celery. Cover tightly and cook on HIGH for 5 to 8 minutes or until the vegetables are tender, stirring once during cooking.

Stir in the remaining ingredients except the tomato juice. Cover tightly and cook on HIGH for 10 to 15 minutes or until boiling; stir. Cover again and cook on MEDIUM for 25 to 30 minutes or until the bulgur is tender and the flavors are blended, stirring after 15 minutes. (Add tomato juice at this point if the mixture seems dry.) Let stand, covered, for 10 minutes.

NOTE: To reheat refrigerated chili, add a little extra tomato juice or water to the chili. Cover tightly and cook on HIGH for 10 minutes; stir. Cover again and cook on MEDIUM for 5 to 15 minutes or until heated through.

*To make an interesting bean combination, substitute 1 can (16 ounces) of garbanzo beans for 1 can (16 ounces) of kidney beans.

Serves: 8

Cooking time: 40 to 50 minutes

2 tablespoons vegetable oil
3 garlic cloves, minced
2 large onions, coarsely chopped
2 green peppers, coarsely chopped
4 celery ribs, coarsely chopped
1 jalapeño pepper, seeded and finely chopped
4 cups peeled and chopped fresh tomatoes or 2 (16-ounce) cans stewed tomatoes
4 cups cooked kidney beans with cooking liquid or 2 (16-ounce) cans, undrained*
1 cup bulgur wheat
2 to 3 tablespoons chili powder
1 tablespoon whole cumin seed or 1 teaspoon ground
1 tablepoon dried oregano
½ teaspoon dried thyme leaves
½ teaspoon salt
¼ teaspoon freshly ground black pepper
Tomato juice (optional), if mixture seems too dry

CINNAMON- AND PAPRIKA-DUSTED CHOCOLATE ICE CREAM BALLS WITH MINTED ENGLISH CREAM

Serves: 12

Cooking time: 3 to 6 minutes

3 quarts good-quality rich dark chocolate
    ice cream
2 tablespoons cinnamon
2 tablespoons paprika

MINTED ENGLISH CREAM:
3 tablespoons sugar
1 tablespoon all-purpose flour
1 cup half-and-half
6 large egg yolks
1 teaspoon vanilla extract or rum
24 fresh mint leaves, stems removed, cut
    into thin strips

Line a cookie sheet with foil. Form 24 ice cream balls with a round or oval ice cream scoop. Place them on the lined cookie sheet. Freeze well.

Combine the cinnamon and paprika in a small bowl. Remove the ice cream balls from the freezer and roll in, or sprinkle with, about ¼ teaspoon of the cinnamon-paprika mixture. Refreeze until serving time.

To make the cream, combine the sugar and flour in a 4-cup glass measure. Stir in the half-and-half. Cook on HIGH for 2 to 4 minutes or until heated but not boiling.

Beat the egg yolks lightly with a fork or whisk in a small bowl to reach a syrup consistency. Add the egg yolks to the half-and-half mixture in a slow, steady stream, beating constantly. Cook on HIGH for 30 seconds to 2 minutes, stirring every 30 seconds until thickened. The sauce may be somewhat coagulated, but a final beating will smooth it out to make a slightly thickened but creamy sauce.

Remove the sauce from the microwave oven, and beat in the vanilla with a whisk. Cool, stirring occasionally to prevent a skin from forming. To speed-cool, place the mixture in the freezer for 30 minutes.

To serve, spoon 2 tablespoons of the cream sauce on each flat dessert plate. Sprinkle each plate with about 1 teaspoon cut-up mint leaves. Arrange 2 ice cream balls on top of each plate.

WARM PINEAPPLE SLICES WITH ORANGE SHERBET

Serves: 12

Cooking time: 4 to 7 minutes

½ cup unsalted butter

1 ripe (3- to 4-pound) pineapple, peeled, cut into quarters lengthwise, with core removed

½ cup brown sugar

1 teaspoon cinnamon

2 tablespoons rum

4 quarts orange sherbet

48 orange segments, from approximately 4 navel oranges

Place the butter in a 2-quart rectangular microwave-proof dish. Cook on HIGH for 1 to 2 minutes to melt.

Meanwhile cut each pineapple quarter into 3 long spears. Add the pineapple spears to the melted butter, turning over to coat all sides. Sprinkle the pineapple, evenly, with the brown sugar, cinnamon, and rum. Cover with wax paper and cook on HIGH for 2 minutes. Turn the slices over and reposition them from inside to outside. Cover again and cook on HIGH for 1 to 3 minutes or until heated through.

To serve, place 1 pineapple spear on each dessert plate with some of the cooking juices spooned over the top. Place 2 small scoops of orange sherbet on each plate and fan out 4 orange segments to the side.

LIME SHERBET WITH TEQUILA

Serves: 16

1 gallon lime sherbet
1 cup tequila

This is a quick dessert that will finish off a Southwestern-style meal. It can easily be doubled or tripled to accommodate a large group.

Place 1 or 2 scoops of lime sherbet in 16 goblets. Spoon about 1 tablespoon tequila into each goblet over the sherbet. Serve.

SERVING SUGGESTION: Rim each glass with salt by moistening the rim in water or lemon juice and then dipping it into coarse salt. Garnish with thin lime slices.

MENU
FOR AN
INDIAN SUMMER
NIGHT

Serves 4

Chilled Creamy Carrot
Soup

Rosemary-Grilled Cornish
Hens

Mango Chutney

"Stir-Fry" of Squashes and
Snow Peas

Rice Pilaf with Pine Nuts

Poached Pear Fans and
Raspberries

Chilled Creamy Carrot
Soup

Rosemary-Grilled Cornish
Hens

Mango Chutney

"Stir-Fry" of Squashes and
Snow Peas

Rice Pilaf with Pine Nuts

Poached Pear Fans and
Raspberries

WINE SUGGESTION
Alsatian white or California
Sauvignon Blanc

Menu
FOR AN
INDIAN SUMMER
NIGHT

A cooling tangerine-colored carrot soup kicks off a meal for one of those hot Indian summer nights. A tangy ginger-mango chutney is the perfect foil to the grilled birds. To round out the meal, serve the rice pilaf with pine nuts and a mélange of barely cooked vegetables. For dessert, poach the season's first pears and serve with raspberries.

PREPARATION PLAN

UP TO 3 DAYS IN ADVANCE:
Make the soup and chutney and poach the pears; refrigerate.

UP TO 2 HOURS IN ADVANCE:
1. Prepare the vegetables for the "stir-fry."
2. Cut the hens in half.

1 HOUR BEFORE SERVING:
1. Cook the pilaf. (Covered, this will keep warm out of the oven until serving time.)
2. Remove the chutney from the refrigerator to bring to room temperature.
3. Preheat the grill and place the hens in the microwave oven. While the hens are cooking for the first 16-minute period, pour and garnish the soup.
4. Serve the soup. (Don't worry if you don't finish the soup by the time the hens are cooked. The microwave oven turns off automatically.)
5. Start cooking the vegetables.
6. Grill the hens and serve with the chutney, rice, and vegetables.

TO SERVE DESSERT:
Slice and fan out pears and garnish.

EVEN EASIER HINTS
Substitute 1 quart good-quality chocolate ice cream and serve with fresh raspberries and purchased cookies.

PARSLEY *Parsley has its roots in Greek and Roman mythology; the French also have long been devoted to parsley, which is a constant component of bouquet garni and fines herbes. ❦ This green plant can be found with flat and curly leaves, and has been used as a perpetual garnish on just about everything. We feel it is at its best when added, cooked or fresh, to a wide number of dishes; stir it in at the end of cooking for a fresh crisp flavor or during cooking as a flavor enhancer.*

CHILLED CREAMY CARROT SOUP

Makes: 4 cups

Cooking time: 6 to 8 minutes

1 garlic clove, minced

1 medium-size onion, chopped

¼ cup orange juice

½ pound carrots, peeled and cut into ½-inch slices

1 medium-size potato, peeled and cut into ½-inch slices

½ cup heavy cream

2 cups chicken broth

¼ teaspoon freshly ground black pepper

⅛ teaspoon cayenne pepper

⅛ teaspoon grated nutmeg

¼ cup chopped fresh chives, plus 24 (2-inch) pieces of chive tops, for garnish

In a 2-quart microwaveproof casserole, combine the garlic, onion, orange juice, carrots, and potato. Cover tightly and cook on HIGH for 6 to 8 minutes or until tender, stirring once.

Puree in a food processor or blender. Pour the cream into the bowl of the food processor, and continue to process until smooth. Return to the casserole and add the broth, black pepper, cayenne, nutmeg, and chopped chives. Stir well and chill for at least 1 hour or up to 4 days.

To serve, divide the soup among four bowls. Arrange 3 pieces of chive tops on top of each bowl of soup.

ROSEMARY-GRILLED CORNISH HENS

The microwave oven and grill pair up to speed the cooking time of the hens and produce the juiciest barbecued hens that you'll ever savor.

Preheat the barbecue grill.

Place the hens breast side up in a 2-quart microwaveproof casserole. Cover with wax paper and cook on HIGH for 8 minutes. Reposition the hens, placing the lesser cooked areas to the outside of the dish. Cover again and cook on HIGH for 8 minutes.

Place the butter in a 1-cup glass measure. Cook on HIGH for 1 minute to melt. Stir in the rosemary. Place the hens, skin side up, on the grill. Baste with the melted rosemary butter. Cook about 4 minutes. Turn the hens over and cook about 4 more minutes or until brown and crisp.

To serve, place half a Cornish hen on each plate, and tuck a small rosemary sprig between each leg and breast section, if desired. If serving chutney, spoon 2 tablespoons of the chutney at the base of each hen and pass the rest.

Serves: 4

Cooking time: 25 minutes

2 Cornish game hens (1½ pounds each), split lengthwise

¼ cup unsalted butter

1 tablespoon fresh rosemary or 1 teaspoon dried

4 sprigs fresh rosemary, for garnish (optional)

Mango Chutney

Makes: 2 cups

Cooking time: 11 minutes

1 garlic clove, minced
2 teaspoons chopped fresh ginger
2 tablespoons cider vinegar
½ cup dark brown sugar
2 ripe mangoes (1 pound each), peeled,
    pitted, and coarsely chopped
½ cup golden raisins
1 tablespoon fresh lime juice
2 teaspoons coarse Dijon mustard
¼ teaspoon salt
⅛ teaspoon cayenne pepper

The wonderful flavors of this chutney enhance any grilled meat, or try it for a snack, spooned on top of yogurt. It is best served at room temperature.

In a 4-cup glass measure, combine the garlic, ginger, vinegar, and brown sugar. Cover with wax paper and cook on HIGH for 3 minutes, stirring once. Stir in the remaining ingredients. Cover again and cook on HIGH for 8 minutes, stirring once. Pour into a serving crock and refrigerate.

NOTE: The chutney will keep refrigerated for up to 1 week.

"STIR-FRY" OF SQUASHES AND SNOW PEAS

Serves: 4

Cooking time: 4 to 5 minutes

1 garlic clove, minced
2 tablespoons unsalted butter
1 tablespoon chopped fresh oregano or
    1 teaspoon dried
½ pound small zucchini, cut into thin
    strips, 2 inches by ¼ inch
½ pound small yellow summer squash,
    cut into thin strips, 2 inches by
    ¼ inch
¼ pound snow pea pods

This is a delicious blend of summer squashes, snow peas, and fresh herbs.

Combine the garlic and butter in a 2-quart rectangular or oval microwaveproof baking dish. Cook on HIGH for 1 minute or until the butter is melted. Add the remaining ingredients and stir to coat with butter. Cover with wax paper and cook on HIGH for 3 to 5 minutes, stirring once until tender-crisp.

RICE PILAF WITH PINE NUTS

Serves: 4

Cooking time: 13 to 19 minutes

2 tablespoons unsalted butter
1 medium-size onion, finely chopped
1 cup long-grain, or converted rice
1¾ cups chicken broth
2 tablespoons chopped fresh parsley
½ cup pine nuts

You must let this rice stand for 5 minutes once the cooking is completed, but it will stay warm for up to an hour, which gives your schedule flexibility.

In a 3-quart microwaveproof casserole combine the butter and onion. Cook on HIGH for 2 to 3 minutes, or until the onion is tender.

Stir in the rice, coating every grain. Stir in the broth. Cover tightly and cook on HIGH for 4 to 6 minutes or until the liquid is boiling; then cook on MEDIUM for 7 to 10 minutes or until most of the liquid has been absorbed and the rice is tender. Stir in the parsley and nuts. Cover and let stand for 5 minutes.

POACHED PEAR FANS AND RASPBERRIES

A good-quality purchased cookie goes well with these fresh-tasting fruits.

In a 2-quart microwaveproof casserole, combine the sugar, wine, vanilla, and lemon juice. Cover tightly and cook on HIGH for 2 to 4 minutes or until the sugar is dissolved. Add the pears to the warm syrup. Cover tightly and cook on HIGH for 8 minutes or until the pears are tender but not too soft, stirring gently once. Chill in the liquid until serving time.

To serve, slice pears every ½ inch from base to top, being careful not to cut through top. Spoon a tablespoon of cooking juices onto each flat dessert plate and fan out pears; sprinkle raspberries randomly on plate.

Variation:

PEAR FANS WITH HOT FUDGE SAUCE: Slice cooled pears, approximately every ½ inch, from base to within 2 inches of stem. Place on a serving plate and fan out. Spoon cooking juices over pears and drizzle with Hot Fudge Sauce (see page 49). Garnish with fresh raspberries and mint leaves if desired.

Serves: 4

Cooking time: 10 to 12 minutes

½ cup sugar
¼ cup dry white wine
1 teaspoon vanilla extract
1 tablepoon lemon juice
4 firm ripe pears, peeled, cored, and cut lengthwise into 16 slices each
½ pint raspberries

BOUNTIFUL PACIFIC NORTHWEST MENU

Serves 6

Fennel and Wild Mushrooms
on Arugula with Warm
Mustard Dressing

Chilled Whole Salmon or
Bass with Cucumber Sauce
and Caviar

Yellow Finnish Potatoes with
Dill

Peas and Snow Peas with
Fresh Mint

Fresh Berries with
Crème Fraîche
or
Apples with Oregon Blue or
Cheddar Cheese

Fennel and Wild Mushrooms
on Arugula with Warm
Mustard Dressing

Chilled Whole Salmon or
Bass with Cucumber Sauce
and Caviar

Yellow Finnish Potatoes with
Dill

Peas and Snow Peas with
Fresh Mint

Fresh Berries with
Crème Fraîche
or
Apples with Oregon Blue or
Cheddar Cheese

WINE SUGGESTION
Northwestern Chardonnay

BOUNTIFUL PACIFIC NORTHWEST MENU

A rainbow of colors! That is what comes to mind when we think of the variety of sumptuous edible riches from the Northwest. ❡ To parade these lush resources, we have planned a menu that opens with a fennel, wild mushroom, and arugula salad, napped with a warm dressing. As a main course, the whole poached fish is easily cooked right on a large serving plate over a bed of parsley, and is best presented this way. Accompany the fish with small yellow Finnish potatoes tossed with butter and dill, and a mélange of peas and snow peas sparked with mint.

PREPARATION PLAN

THE DAY BEFORE:

Cook the salmon or bass and cucumber sauce; cover and refrigerate.

1 HOUR BEFORE SERVING:

1. Prepare the peas and snow peas for cooking.
2. Cut the cheese into small individual wedges, if serving.
3. Wash and dry the arugula; prepare the fennel and mushrooms, and arrange the salad plates.
4. Mix up the salad dressing and set aside.
5. Prepare the potatoes and cook. Set aside, covered, until ready to serve. (They will keep warm for a long time.)
6. Spoon the sauce on the chilled salmon and sprinkle with the caviar.

AT THE TABLE:

1. Heat the salad dressing and serve the salad.
2. Clear the salad course and cook the peas and snow peas.
3. Serve the salmon with the peas and potatoes.
4. After removing the main course, cut up apple wedges to serve with cheese or spoon out berries and pass a bowl of crème fraîche.

DILL *A plant in the parsley family, dill has seeds and leaves with various uses. The feathery leaves delicately brighten sauces, green beans, cucumbers, and breads. And one can hardly think of salmon without linking it to dill leaves, especially in Scandinavian "gravlax." ❡ The dill blossoms are large, round disks made up of many small white flowers that produce dill seeds. These are more pungent than the leaves and are most commonly used in pickling (said to aid in the digestion of cucumbers) and as an addition to cooked cabbage and potato salads.*

FENNEL AND WILD MUSHROOMS ON ARUGULA WITH WARM MUSTARD DRESSING

Serves: 6

Cooking time: 2 minutes

1 bunch arugula, carefully washed
2 cups thinly sliced fennel stalks
12 ounces fresh wild mushrooms
   (shiitake, chanterelle, or oyster
   mushrooms, or a mixture), cleaned
   and sliced
¼ cup olive oil
4 green onions, thinly sliced
2 tablespoons red wine vinegar
1 teaspoon Dijon mustard with seeds
¼ teaspoon salt
¼ teaspoon freshly ground black pepper
2 tablespoons toasted pine nuts

Arrange the arugula on six serving plates. In a bowl, toss together the fennel and mushrooms. Divide evenly on top of the arugula.

In a 2-cup glass measure, combine the oil and onions. Cook on HIGH for 40 seconds. Stir in the vinegar, mustard, salt, and pepper. Cook on HIGH for 1 minute. Spoon over the salads and sprinkle with the pine nuts.

CHILLED WHOLE SALMON OR BASS WITH CUCUMBER SAUCE AND CAVIAR

Serves: 6

Cooking time: 14 to 17 minutes

20 sprigs parsley
1 (3-pound) whole salmon or bass,
    cleaned, with head and tail intact
¼ cup dry white wine or vermouth

SAUCE:
1 pound cucumbers, peeled, seeded, and
    thinly sliced into crescents
1 tablespoon lemon juice
1 tablespoon chopped chives
1 tablespoon chopped dill
1 teaspoon grated lemon rind
¼ teaspoon salt
¼ teaspoon freshly ground black pepper
½ cup sour cream
1 cup plain yogurt

½ cup salmon caviar

Arrange the parsley sprigs on a 3-quart microwave-proof serving platter or rectangular dish. Place the salmon on top, allowing the parsley to protrude to form a lacy edge around the fish. Pour the wine over the fish. Cover tightly with plastic wrap turned back slightly on one side. Cook on MEDIUM for 12 to 15 minutes or until the fish flakes in the thickest part when pressed with a finger or fork, rotating the dish one-quarter turn twice. Chill for 2 hours on the platter.

To make sauce: Place the cucumbers in a 1-quart microwaveproof casserole. Cover tightly and cook on HIGH for 2 minutes, stirring halfway through the cooking. Rinse under cold water and drain well. Combine the drained cucumbers and the remaining ingredients, except the caviar, in a medium bowl and mix well. Chill until serving time.

Serve the salmon drizzled with a ribbon of sauce and sprinkled with the caviar. Serve the remaining sauce on the side.

YELLOW FINNISH POTATOES WITH DILL

Serves: 6

Cooking time: 9 to 11 minutes

1½ pounds yellow Finnish (or substitute small red) potatoes, washed, with a strip peeled around the middle
¼ cup unsalted butter
2 tablespoons chopped fresh dill

Combine the potatoes and butter in a 2-quart microwaveproof casserole. Cover tightly and cook on HIGH for 6 to 8 minutes or until tender, stirring once after 3 minutes. Let stand, covered, for 3 minutes. Sprinkle with the dill and stir to coat.

PEAS AND SNOW PEAS WITH FRESH MINT

Serves: 6

Cooking time: 5 to 9 minutes

2 tablespoons unsalted butter
¼ cup thinly sliced green onions
1 cup fresh peas or frozen, broken up
¼ pound snow peas, trimmed and cut into 1-inch diagonals
1 tablespoon chopped fresh mint

Combine the butter and green onions in a 1-quart microwaveproof casserole. Cook on HIGH for 1 minute. Stir in the peas. Cover tightly and cook on HIGH for 2 minutes. Stir in the snow peas. Cover again and cook on HIGH for 2 to 4 minutes or until the snow peas are tender-crisp. Sprinkle with the fresh mint and serve.

FRESH BERRIES WITH CRÈME FRAÎCHE

Serves: 6

Right before serving rinse berries and divide them among six serving bowls. Top with a little crème fraîche and garnish with a mint leaf.

2 pints fully ripe berries (blackberries, raspberries, strawberries, or blueberries; a combination of two is nice)
2 cups crème fraîche
Mint leaves, for garnish

APPLES WITH OREGON BLUE OR CHEDDAR CHEESE

Plan on having enough apples so that everyone can taste at least an apple half from each variety. A nice Northwest combination would be Golden Delicious, Granny Smith, Red Delicious, and when available, "Blushing" Granny Smith. Figure on about ¾ pound of cheese, even though most people will only want about an ounce.

MEDITERRANEAN DINNER IN MID-MARCH

Serves 6

Warm Caponata

Mediterranean Fish Stew
with Aïoli

Crusty Garlic Bread

Pine Nut–Crusted Cheese
Pie with Fresh Fruits

Sambuca-Espresso Truffles

MEDITERRANEAN DINNER IN MID-MARCH

*A*t this time of year *our thoughts turn to the warmer Mediterranean coast. With a fire crackling in the fireplace, we study the travel section of our newspaper and try to capture the spirit in our kitchens.* ❦ *A menu that begins with an olive and tomato caponata seems appropriate—it may be prepared an hour or so before serving, then mounded on lettuce-lined plates as a first-course salad. The lemony cheese pie and even the broth for the fish stew may be assembled and cooked in advance, but don't add the fish until you are ready to serve the caponata. This will assure the freshest flavor and texture of the fish possible.*

PREPARATION PLAN

THE DAY BEFORE OR EARLIER IN THE DAY:
1. Make the cheese pie and refrigerate.
2. Make the truffles (see page 36) and refrigerate.

EARLIER IN THE DAY:
1. Cook the caponata and refrigerate.
2. Prepare the garlic bread.
3. Make the aïoli and refrigerate.

1 HOUR BEFORE SERVING:
1. Prepare the broth for the stew.
2. Line the salad plates with the greens and cut up the pepper.

30 MINUTES BEFORE SERVING:
1. Reheat the fish stew broth for 6 to 8 minutes or until boiling.
2. Preheat the conventional oven for the garlic bread.

3. Add the squid and fish to the broth and serve the caponata.

AT THE TABLE:
1. While clearing the caponata plates, place the garlic bread in the conventional oven.
2. Add the mussels and shrimp to the stew.
3. Serve the stew with aïoli and bread.
4. While preparing coffee (espresso is nice with this menu) or tea, garnish the cheese pie and put out the truffles.

EVEN EASIER HINTS
Substitute Parmigiano Reggiano cheese and ripe pears or grapes for the cheese pie.

CAPERS *The caper plant is an ornamental one that adds distinction to the walls and cliffs of southern France, the Mediterranean region, Algeria, Turkey, and parts of Asia. The flowers are especially striking with large white petals and numerous long stamens. The fruit is a dry spongy berry full of black seeds, and it is fruit from the young plants (flowers not yet open) that are the base for pickled capers.*
❦ *These pickled seeds are slightly bitter and contain a substance with tonic and diuretic properties. They add a unique flavor to salads, sauces, appetizers, and certain meats. The young seeds of the nasturtium can also be pickled and used in the same way as capers.*

WARM CAPONATA

Serves: 6

Cooking time: About 15 minutes

½ cup olive oil

2 medium-size onions, thinly sliced

1 garlic clove, minced

2 medium-size tomatoes, peeled and
  chopped

2 celery ribs, diced

2 medium-size eggplant, peeled and diced

1 green pepper, stem and membrane
  removed, diced

6 bottled Italian olives, pitted and cut
  into quarters

2 tablespoons red wine vinegar

1 tablespoon sugar

1 teaspoon dried crushed oregano

½ teaspoon salt

¼ teaspoon freshly ground black pepper

¼ cup capers, drained

Arugula, romaine, or watercress leaves

1 yellow pepper, thinly sliced lengthwise,
  for garnish

Sweet and tart—a delicious warm salad.

In a 2-quart microwaveproof casserole, combine the oil, onions, and garlic. Cover with the lid or plastic wrap turned back slightly on one side, and cook on HIGH for 2 minutes or until the onions are slightly tender.

Stir in the remaining ingredients except the capers, arugula, and yellow pepper. Cover again and cook on HIGH for 8 minutes; stir well. Re-cover and cook on HIGH for 4 to 6 minutes or until the vegetables are tender and the flavors are developed.

Stir in the capers. Let stand at room temperature for 1 hour. If not serving immediately, refrigerate. When ready to serve, reheat on HIGH for 3 to 4 minutes, until just slightly warm, stirring once.

To serve, line six salad plates with arugula, romaine, or watercress leaves. Spoon the caponata onto the greens and fan out the yellow pepper slices around the rims of the plates.

MEDITERRANEAN FISH STEW WITH AÏOLI

Serves: 6

Cooking time: 17 to 23 minutes

In a 3-quart microwaveproof casserole, combine the oil, garlic, and onion. Cover tightly with the lid or plastic wrap turned back slightly on one side, and cook on HIGH for 2 minutes. Add the tomatoes, water, wine, basil, parsley, salt, black and red peppers, and bay leaf. Cover again and cook on HIGH for 6 to 8 minutes or until boiling; stir.

Add the squid and fish. Cover again and cook on HIGH for 7 to 9 minutes or until the fish becomes opaque, stirring halfway through the cooking.

Arrange the mussels and shrimp around the outer rim of the casserole. Re-cover and cook on HIGH for 2 to 4 minutes or until the mussels are open and the shrimp pink. Ladle into soup bowls and serve with aïoli and crusty French or Italian bread or garlic bread, for absorbing the wonderful cooking juices.

¼ cup olive oil

2 garlic cloves, minced

1 onion, finely chopped

1½ cups peeled, seeded, and chopped ripe tomatoes (preferably plum) or canned, undrained and chopped

1 cup water

¼ cup dry white wine

¼ cup chopped fresh basil or 1 teaspoon dried

¼ cup choppped fresh parsley

½ teaspoon salt

½ teaspoon freshly ground black pepper

⅛ teaspoon dried red pepper flakes

1 bay leaf, crushed

1 pound squid, dressed and rinsed well, cut into ¼-inch circles, including tentacles (or substitute ½ pound fish fillets)

2 pounds assorted thick, lean fish fillets, cut into 1½-inch pieces (such as whiting, halibut, monkfish, bass)

1 dozen mussels, debearded and scrubbed

½ pound shrimp, shelled and deveined

Aïoli (recipe follows)

TO CLEAN SQUID

Cut the tentacles off of the squid, in front of the eyes, reserving the tentacles. Remove the quill-like skeleton from the sac, then remove the viscera (internal organs) and discard. Wash out the inside of the sac, removing any missed parts. Peel off the outer skin of the squid under cold running water. Dry thoroughly.

97

AÏOLI (GARLIC MAYONNAISE)

Makes: About 2 cups

4 to 6 garlic cloves, finely minced
1 tablespoon lemon juice
2 tablespoons dry bread crumbs
4 large egg yolks
1½ cups oil, 1 cup olive oil and ½ cup
    vegetable oil (preferred)
¼ teaspoon salt
Dash cayenne pepper (optional)

Processor Method: In the bowl of a food processor, combine garlic, lemon juice, bread crumbs, and egg yolks; process until thoroughly mixed. As the processor is running, add oil in a slow, steady stream. Once oil has been added, the mixture will begin to thicken. When all oil has been added, season to taste and process lightly.

Hand Method: In a medium-size bowl, combine bread crumbs and lemon juice; mix into a paste with a wooden spoon. Add garlic and egg yolks to bread-crumb mixture. Add oil in a slow, steady stream, beating constantly with a whisk or spoon until thick. Season to taste. Keep refrigerated.

CRUSTY GARLIC BREAD

Serves: 6

Cooking time: 2 to 3 minutes

2 (12- to 14-inch) loaves crusty Italian
    bread
½ cup unsalted butter
2 garlic cloves, finely chopped

Cut the bread in half lengthwise. Place the butter into a 1-cup glass measure with the garlic. Cook on HIGH for 1 to 2 minutes, until butter is melted. Brush the butter and garlic onto the cut surfaces of the bread.

Place the cut side of each loaf of bread together. To heat bread in conventional oven: preheat oven to 400°F. Wrap in foil and heat bread for 15 minutes or until warmed throughout.

Variation:
FOR GRILLED GARLIC BREAD: Prepare as above, place buttered sides down on heated grill for 1 to 2 minutes to toast—nice for a barbecue.

PINE NUT–CRUSTED CHEESE PIE WITH FRESH FRUITS

To make the crust, place the butter in a 9-inch glass pie plate. Cook on HIGH for 1 to 1½ minutes or until melted. Stir in the cookie crumbs and pine nuts until well blended. Press firmly against the bottom and sides of the dish to form a crust. Cook on HIGH for 1½ to 2½ minutes or until set, rotating the dish once. Set aside.

To make the filling, in an 8-cup glass measure, combine the ricotta, sour cream, sugar, flour, lemon rind, and eggs. Cook on HIGH for 6 to 10 minutes or until the center is very warm to the touch, stirring every 2 minutes. (The mixture will be a little lumpy at this point, but it will cook into a smooth pie.) Pour the filling into the crust, smoothing it evenly on top.

Place the pie on top of a microwaveproof cereal bowl in the microwave oven. Cook on MEDIUM for 8 to 14 minutes or until almost set in the center, rotating one-quarter turn once or twice. Let stand directly on the counter for 30 minutes.

Chill for 3 hours or overnight before serving. Garnish the pie with berries, small bunches of grapes, or orange segments.

Serves: 6 to 8

Cooking time: 16 to 28 minutes

PINE NUT CRUST:

¼ cup unsalted butter

¾ cup crumbs made from amaretti or other almond-flavored cookies

½ cup pine nuts

CHEESE FILLING:

15 ounces ricotta cheese

1 cup sour cream

½ cup sugar

2 tablespoons all-purpose flour

2 teaspoons grated lemon rind

2 large eggs, beaten

Fresh berries, small bunches of grapes, or orange segments, for garnish

HOT
AUGUST NIGHT

Serves 4

Warm Corn-and-Pepper
Salad

Spicy Shrimp in Wine

Crusty French Bread

Fresh Peach Slices with
Zabaglione

Espresso

HOT
AUGUST NIGHT

Duing the lazy, hazy days of summer, we like to plan meals that show off the bounty of the season but take a minimum of effort. This light supper can be prepared and served in less than an hour, even when moving at an August pace. ❡ Even the salad can be whipped up in advance, and most of the work involved with the shrimp is done by participants as your guests peel their own. Luxuriant warm hand towels are the reward for those efforts. Serve plenty of crusty bread for dunking in the shrimp broth. A good strong espresso is delicious with the zabaglione.

PREPARATION PLAN

1 HOUR BEFORE SERVING:

1. Prepare the greens and cook the vegetables for the salad.
2. Blanch, peel, and slice the peaches into the serving glasses.
3. Assemble the ingredients for the zabaglione.
4. Assemble the ingredients for the shrimp.
5. Prepare the towels and arrange in the basket. Cover with plastic wrap.

10 MINUTES BEFORE SERVING:

Cook the shrimp.

AT THE TABLE:

1. While the shrimp are cooking, arrange the salads and serve.
2. Serve the shrimp.
3. Clear the shrimp course and heat the towels.
4. Make the espresso, if desired.

5. While the towels are being enjoyed, whisk up the zabaglione and serve over the peaches.

EVEN EASIER HINTS

Substitute a good French vanilla ice cream for the zabaglione.

CUTTING CALORIES

Eliminate the zabaglione and add 3 sliced plums and 1 peeled and sliced papaya to the peaches.

WARM SCENTED FINGER TOWELS *Combine 2 tablespoons lemon juice with 2 cups water. Wet 4 washcloths in this water, wring out, and roll. Tie each with a cloth ribbon and place into a wicker basket with no metal staples. Cover with plastic wrap to keep moist until ready to heat. Keep covered and heat on* HIGH *1 to 2 minutes or until warm.*

WARM CORN-AND-PEPPER SALAD

Serves: 4

Cooking time: 4 to 5 minutes

2 tablespoons olive oil
1 garlic clove, minced
1 medium-size onion, chopped
2 cups fresh corn kernels
1 green pepper, trimmed, seeded, and
    diced
1 sweet red pepper, trimmed, seeded, and
    diced
2 teaspoons balsamic vinegar
¼ teaspoon salt
¼ teaspoon freshly ground black pepper
2 fresh basil leaves, minced
4 cups mixed salad greens, such as
    arugula and red-tipped lettuce

In a 2-quart microwaveproof casserole, combine the oil, garlic, onion, corn, and red and green peppers. Cover tightly with the lid or plastic wrap turned back slightly on one side, and cook on HIGH for 4 to 5 minutes or until tender-crisp, stirring once.

Stir in the remaininng ingredients except the greens. Let stand, covered, at room temperature until serving time.

To serve, line four salad plates with the greens. Spoon some warm salad into the center of each plate.

SPICY SHRIMP IN WINE

Serves: 4

Cooking time: 8 to 13 minutes

½ cup unsalted butter
2 garlic cloves, minced
1 cup dry white wine
1 tablespoon lemon juice

In a 2-quart round microwaveproof casserole, combine the butter and garlic. Cook on HIGH for 1 to 2 minutes or until the butter is melted. Add the wine and cook on HIGH for 2 to 3 minutes or until boiling.

Add the remaining ingredients except the parsley. Stir to coat the shrimp, then push the shrimp to the outer rim of the dish, leaving the center open. Cover tightly with the lid or plastic wrap turned back slightly on one side, and cook on HIGH for 5 to 8 minutes or until the shrimp turn pink and test done, stirring after 3 minutes. Let stand, covered, for 2 to 3 minutes.

Divide the shrimp and cooking juices among four bowls to serve. Sprinkle with the parsley.

1 teaspoon Worcestershire sauce
½ teaspoon salt
½ teaspoon crushed hot pepper
½ teaspoon dried thyme
¼ teaspoon cayenne pepper
1½ pounds medium-size shrimp, washed but not peeled
¼ cup chopped fresh parsley

FRESH PEACH SLICES WITH ZABAGLIONE

Divide the fruit among four large wine glasses.
Place the egg yolks in a 1-quart microwaveproof casserole; beat lightly with a wire whisk. Gradually add the sugar, beating with the whisk to blend. Cook on MEDIUM for 1 to 2 minutes or until the mixture is partially cooked around the edges. Whip well with the whisk to incorporate air and until smooth. Whisk in the wine. Cook on MEDIUM for 1 to 1½ minutes more or until thickened, whipping ever 30 seconds. Remove from the microwave oven and beat with the whisk for 30 seconds or so, until the mixture is fluffy.

To serve, spoon the zabaglione over the peaches.

Serves: 4

Cooking time: 2 to 3½ minutes

3 fresh peaches, blanched, peeled, and cut into slices (see Note)
4 large egg yolks
¼ cup sugar
¼ cup Marsala wine

NOTE: To blanch and peel the peaches, pour 1 cup water into a 2-quart microwaveproof casserole or glass measure. Cook on HIGH for 2 to 3 minutes to boil. Add the peaches. Cover tightly with the lid or plastic wrap turned back slightly on one side, and cook on HIGH for 2 minutes, turning peaches over after 1 minute. Remove peaches, rinse in cold water, and peel. The peach skins impart a lovely rosy glow to the flesh of the fruit when blanched in this manner.

HOMESPUN BARBECUED RIB DINNER

Serves 6

Marinated Vegetables in
Jelly Jars

Spiced Nuts Under Glass

Mesquite Barbecued Ribs
with
A Pinch-of-Soul Barbecue
Sauce

Warm Black-Eyed Pea
Salad
or
Potato Salad with Fennel

Grilled Corn

Corn Bread

Brownie Pie

Ice Cream with Warm
Blueberry Sauce

HOMESPUN BARBECUED RIB DINNER

These Mesquite Barbecued Ribs have all the appeal of a rack torched in a smoky pit in west Texas but in a fraction of the time and trouble. The secret method is precooking the ribs in the microwave oven before grilling. This allows for pinpoint timing and foolproof results; these ribs will be delicious every time. ❦ Serve the barbecue sauce as a condiment at the table. It whispers "hot" just loud enough to summon pitchers of refreshing iced tea or ice-cold beer.

BEVERAGE SUGGESTION
Beer or iced tea

PREPARATION PLAN

THE DAY BEFORE:
1. Make the marinated vegetables and refrigerate; make the spiced nuts.
2. Make the barbecue sauce and salads; refrigerate.
3. Make the corn bread.

EARLIER IN THE DAY:
Make the brownie pie and, after cooling, keep covered.

1 HOUR 30 MINUTES BEFORE SERVING:
1. Begin cooking the ribs in the microwave oven and heat the grill.
2. Take the marinated vegetables from the refrigerator and let them come to room temperature.
3. Take the salads from the refrigerator and let stand at room temperature.

AT THE TABLE:
1. Serve the marinated vegetables and nuts on a tray while the ribs are cooking for the last half-hour.
2. Cook the ribs on the grill.
3. Cook the corn in the microwave oven, then transfer to the grill.
4. When the ribs and corn are cooked, served with the salads and corn bread.
5. Cook blueberry sauce.
6. Top brownie pie with ice cream and sauce.

EVEN EASIER HINTS
1. Buy corn bread, sourdough bread, or crusty bread instead of making the corn bread.
2. Serve the ice cream with raspberries and blueberries instead of the blueberry sauce.

SHALLOT *The origin of the shallot is unknown because it has never been found in the wild. It is believed to be derived from the onion, and looks like something between an onion and a garlic clove in size and in color. In fact, it may embody the best attributes of garlic, onion, and scallion all rolled into one. It is indispensable to French cooking and is a superb addition to a simple vinaigrette dressing.*

MARINATED VEGETABLES IN JELLY JARS

Serves: 6

Cooking time: 14 minutes

4 glass jelly jars with lids (each about 3 inches high)

MARINADE:

¼ cup white wine

3 tablespoons olive oil

2 tablespoons lemon juice

1 tablespoon chopped shallot or sliced green onion

¼ teaspoon salt

Freshly ground black pepper

1 teaspoon chopped fresh thyme, plus 1 sprig for garnish

1 teaspoon chopped fresh basil, plus 1 sprig for garnish

1 teaspoon chopped fresh dill, plus 1 sprig for garnish

VEGETABLES:

2 cups sliced mushrooms

½ pound whole green snap beans, ends removed

1 red bell pepper, cut into ¼-inch-thick lengths

1 green or yellow bell pepper, cut into ¼-inch-thick lengths

2 large carrots, washed and cut into 2-inch-long sticks

Each herb-scented vegetable sparkles in its own attractive jar, which also makes them ideal for an easy-to-pack appetizer or vegetable for a picnic.

Wash the jelly jars and set aside.

Combine all the marinade ingredients except the herbs in a 4-cup glass measure. Add the mushrooms. Cook on HIGH for 2 minutes, stirring once halfway through the cooking. Remove the mushrooms with a slotted spoon and place in the first jelly jar.

Add the green beans to the liquid. Cover with plastic wrap turned back on one side, and cook on HIGH for 4 minutes, stirring once halfway through the cooking. Remove the beans in the same manner as for the mushrooms and stand them upright in another jar. Sprinkle with the chopped thyme.

Add the peppers to the liquid; cover again and cook on HIGH for 4 minutes, stirring halfway through the cooking. Remove the peppers and stand them upright in another jar. Sprinkle with the chopped basil.

Add the carrots to the liquid; cover again and cook on HIGH for 4 minutes, stirring halfway through the cooking. Remove the carrots and stand them upright in the last jar. Sprinkle with the chopped dill.

Divide the remaining marinade among the jars, pouring it over the vegetables. To garnish, slip a sprig of the accompanying herb for each into the side of its jar and cover with the lid. Chill for at least 1 hour.

NOTE: To quickly bring to room temperature, remove the chilled vegetables from the refrigerator and remove the lids. Place the jars in the microwave oven and heat on HIGH for 2 to 3 minutes.

SPICED NUTS UNDER GLASS

Present these to guests in one or two attractive jelly jars for nibbling with drinks before dinner.

Place the butter in a 2-quart rectangular microwave-proof dish. Cook on HIGH for 1 to 2 minutes or until melted. Stir in the remaining ingredients except the nuts.

Stir in the nuts, coating well. Cook, uncovered, on HIGH for 6 to 8 minutes or until heated through, stirring halfway through the cooking. Cool. Place in jelly jars and seal tightly at room temperature. These keep for about 1 month.

Makes: 2 cups

Cooking time: 7 to 10 minutes

¼ cup unsalted butter
2 tablespoons Worcestershire sauce
1 teaspoon Tabasco
½ teaspoon salt
½ teaspoon ground cinnamon
Pinch garlic powder
Pinch ground cloves
2 cups shelled whole pecans, almonds, or
    walnuts, or a mixture

PACK AS A PICNIC

This is the type of menu that can be packed up for a picnic-barbecue. Even the ribs can be precooked and wrapped in foil to keep warm for the final cooking on a grill at the picnic grounds or beach. ❦ For a pretty presentation, each jar lid on the vegetables and nuts can be covered with a bit of fabric—checks or country flowers are good—and tied with a ribbon. The salads travel well in plastic containers and the corn bread and brownies can be left in their cooking dishes. Take along some fresh blueberries to eat plain or with the brownies.

111

MESQUITE BARBECUED RIBS

Serves: 6

Cooking time: 1 hour and 25 minutes

6 pounds pork spareribs, cut into 8 sections
2 handfuls soaked mesquite chips
A Pinch-of-Soul Barbecue Sauce (recipe follows)

In a 2-quart rectangular microwaveproof dish, place half the ribs, meaty side down, with the thicker sections to the outside (overlapping will be necessary). Cover with wax paper. Cook on HIGH for 5 minutes; then cook on MEDIUM for 10 minutes per pound, turning over and rearranging halfway through the cooking. Transfer to a platter and set aside.

Drain the juices from the cooked ribs. Follow the same procedure with the remaining ribs.

Meanwhile, heat the grill and scatter the soaked chips over the coals just before grilling the ribs. Grill the ribs for 5 minutes per side, basting two or three times with some sauce.

Serve the ribs with the sauce at the table.

A PINCH-OF-SOUL BARBECUE SAUCE

Makes: 2 cups

Cooking time: 10 to 11 minutes

2 tablespoons unsalted butter
2 garlic cloves, minced
1 large onion, finely chopped
1 cup ketchup
¼ cup brown sugar
¼ cup cider vinegar
2 tablespoons soy sauce
2 tablespoons Worcestershire sauce
¼ teaspoon cayenne pepper

In a 4-cup glass measure, combine the butter, garlic, and onion. Cook on HIGH for 3 to 4 minutes or until tender. Stir in the remaining ingredients and cook on HIGH for 7 minutes, stirring once. Serve at the table, warm or at room temperature.

WARM BLACK-EYED PEA SALAD

The peanut oil gives this southern salad a nutty flavor.

Serves: 6

Cooking time: 13 to 17 minutes

In a 1½-quart microwaveproof casserole, combine the oil and onion. Cook on HIGH for 1 minute.

Stir in the remaining ingredients except the parsley, sprouts, and tomatoes. Cover tightly with the lid or plastic wrap turned back slightly on one side, and cook on HIGH for 5 to 7 minutes or until the liquid boils; stir. Cover again and cook on MEDIUM for 8 to 10 minutes or until the peas are tender but still crisp. Let stand, covered, for 5 minutes.

Stir in the parsley and correct the seasonings. Spoon onto a serving plate and garnish with a ring of sprouts and tomatoes. Serve warm or at room temperature.

⅓ cup peanut oil or vegetable oil
1 medium-size onion, chopped
3 cups shelled black-eyed peas
3 tablespoons red wine vinegar
½ teaspoon salt
¼ teaspoon thyme leaves
⅛ teaspoon red pepper flakes
Pinch freshly ground black pepper
¼ cup chopped fresh parsley
Radish sprouts or clover, for garnish
12 plum tomatoes, for garnish

FOR A KIDS AND ADULTS' PARTY

Kids' birthdays and other special occasions like the Fourth of July call for parties for kids and parents together. This meal would be perfect for that with just some minor changes. The marinated vegetables in jars are probably best left without the final dressing addition (if your kids are like our little ones, they tend to get their oily hands on all sorts of things). The potato salad will be more popular than the black-eyed pea salad, and 6 ears of fresh corn cooked and cut up into 3 pieces each will be more popular than the corn bread.

POTATO SALAD WITH FENNEL

Serves: 6

Cooking time: 10 to 12 minutes

1½ pounds new or long white potatoes, washed

¼ cup water

⅓ cup vegetable or olive oil

2 tablespoons vinegar

½ teaspoon salt

¼ teaspoon freshly ground black pepper

2 tablespoons finely chopped scallion, chives, or onion

2 tablespoons chopped fresh parsley

¾ cup mayonnaise

¾ cup thinly sliced fennel root or celery, feathery tops reserved for garnish

The fennel adds a light licorice flavor to this salad.

Pierce the potatoes. Place them in a 3-quart microwaveproof casserole. Add the water. Cover tightly and cook on HIGH for 10 to 12 minutes or until tender, turning over and repositioning them (put the ones on the outside inside and vice versa) halfway through the cooking. Let stand, covered, for 10 minutes or until they can be handled.

Drain and cool. Peel and cut the potatoes into large cubes; place in a serving bowl.

In a small mixing bowl, combine the oil, vinegar, salt, and pepper. Pour over the warm potatoes. Let marinate for at least 30 minutes at room temperature. Stir in the remaining ingredients except the fennel tops just before serving. Garnish with some of the feathery fennel tops.

GRILLED CORN

Serves: 6

Cooking time: About 12 minutes

6 large ears corn, husked
¼ cup water
2 tablespoons unsalted butter, melted (optional)

Combine the corn and water in a 2-quart rectangular microwaveproof dish. Cover tightly with plastic wrap turned back slightly on one side. Cook on HIGH for 10 to 12 minutes, rotating the dish once during the cooking, until just tender.

Place the corn on the preheated grill over medium-hot coals. (The coals should be ash-gray with no flame.) Brush the corn with butter, if desired. Cook on the grill for 1 to 2 minutes, turning once (the corn is already cooked; this is just to give it a little golden color and grilled flavor).

NOTE: To simplify, cook and serve corn on a 10- to 12-inch oval microwaveproof plate.

CORN BREAD

Serves: 12

Cooking time: 21 to 28 minutes

¼ cup unsalted butter, melted
1 cup yellow cornmeal
1 cup all-purpose flour
¼ cup sugar
3 teaspoons baking powder
¼ teaspoon salt
1 cup buttermilk
1 egg, slightly beaten

We like to bake this bread in our conventional oven while using our microwave oven for the things it cooks best. The microwave oven is used for melting the butter.

Place the butter into a 1-cup glass measure. Cook on HIGH for 1 to 2 minutes, until melted.

Preheat oven to 400°F. Grease a square baking pan (9 × 9 × 2 inch).

Meanwhile, combine cornmeal, flour, sugar, baking powder, and salt in bowl. Stir in buttermilk, egg, and melted butter and mix gently until just combined.

Pour batter into the greased pan and bake for 20 to 25 minutes, until edges are lightly browned and a knife inserted in the center comes out clean. To serve, cut into 12 pieces and place into a napkin-lined basket.

BROWNIE PIE

Serves: 6 to 8

Cooking time: 14 to 16 minutes

3 large eggs, at room temperature
½ cup granulated sugar
½ cup brown sugar
1 teaspoon vanilla extract
2 ounces unsweetened chocolate
2 ounces semisweet chocolate
½ cup unsalted butter
⅔ cup all-purpose flour
½ cup coarsely chopped walnuts
1 quart vanilla ice cream
1 ounce coarsely grated semisweet
    chocolate

A dense and delicious brownie made even more sinful by adding a scoop of ice cream with chocolate shavings, or Poached Pear Fans and Raspberries (see page 83).

With a mixer, beat the eggs, sugars, and vanilla together for about 8 minutes or until light and doubled in volume.

Meanwhile, place the chocolate squares and butter in a 4-cup glass measure. Melt on HIGH for 3 to 4 minutes or until melted.

Fold the chocolate-butter mixture into the egg mixture. Fold in the flour and nuts. Pour into a 10-inch glass pie plate and smooth the top evenly with a spatula.

Place an inverted cereal bowl in the microwave oven and place the pie on top. Cook, uncovered, on MEDIUM for 8 minutes, then on HIGH for 3 to 4 minutes or until a toothpick comes out clean. Let stand directly on the counter for 10 to 20 minutes. (If not serving until the following day, cover tightly with plastic wrap to keep fresh and moist.)

Right before serving, cut into wedges and top each wedge with a scoop of ice cream and sprinkle with the coarsely grated chocolate.

ICE CREAM WITH BLUEBERRY SAUCE

This is a good dessert for the Fourth of July because it flags the red, white, and blue.

To serve, scoop the ice cream into bowls and ladle the sauce on top. Insert a little American flag into the top of each.

Serves: 6

Cooking time: 11 to 14 minutes

½ gallon ice cream
Warm Blueberry Sauce (see page 179)

CALIFORNIA-STYLE FISH FILLET DINNER

Serves 4

Crudités with Lime-Cayenne
Hollandaise

Fish Fillets in Spinach Nests
with Fresh Tomato-Tarragon
Coulis

Barley Pilaf with Sunflower
Seeds and Radicchio

Poached Figs with White
Chocolate Anglaise

WINE SUGGESTION
Sauvignon Blanc or
Chardonnay

CALIFORNIA-STYLE FISH FILLET DINNER

Satisfying in its texture and flavor combinations, but not heavy, this menu reminds us of all the good things about eating in California—with the emphasis on fresh. ❦ It begins with simple raw vegetables—crudités—and a zesty hollandaise dipping sauce. An earthy grain pilaf follows with flounder fillets curled into spinach mounds, caressed by a delicate creamy tomato sauce. And who can resist a chocolate dessert? Especially this one that features a pool of white chocolate to reflect succulent poached figs.

PREPARATION PLAN

THE DAY BEFORE:

1. Make the poached figs and White Chocolate Anglaise and refrigerate.
2. Make the hollandaise sauce and chill.
3. Wash and trim spinach. Refrigerate in plastic bag.

1½ HOURS BEFORE SERVING:

1. Make the barley pilaf and let sit, covered, after cooking. It will keep warm for up to an hour.
2. Cut up the ingredients for the coulis.
3. Cut up the crudités for the dip and arrange on a platter to serve.

AT THE TABLE:

1. While the guests are eating the crudités, cook the fish and coulis.
2. Serve the fish, spinach, and coulis with a portion of barley pilaf.
3. Serve the poached figs and White Chocolate Anglaise.

EVEN EASIER HINTS

Instead of poaching the figs, serve them fresh (cut in half) in the anglaise sauce. You will need fully ripened figs for this.

TARRAGON *Tarragon has a distinctive aroma, with a slight touch of licorice. It should be used sparingly. As it is best when fresh, we keep pots on our kitchen windowsills in fall and winter and then move them outside for spring and summer. It gives stew a wonderfully distinctive flavor and a touch added to salad is delightful. ❡ If you have any to spare, make tarragon vinegar by combining 1 cup fresh whole tarragon in a glass bottle with 1 quart good-quality cider, red, or white wine vinegar (a 1 to 4 ratio). Store at room temperature for 2 to 4 weeks.*

CRUDITÉS WITH LIME-CAYENNE HOLLANDAISE

Makes: 1 cup

Cooking time: About 3 minutes

SAUCE:

¼ pound unsalted butter

1 tablespoon water

2 tablespoons lime juice

3 egg yolks, beaten

1 teaspoon grated lime rind

¼ teaspoon cayenne pepper

VEGETABLES:

2 medium-size carrots, peeled and cut
    into matchsticks

½ medium-size cauliflower, broken into
    flowerets

1 green or red bell pepper, seeded and cut
    into rings or slices

The selection suggested here may be substituted by any raw vegetables of your choice. You may want to serve this delicious sauce with grilled or smoked fish.

To make the sauce, place the butter in a 4-cup glass measure. Cook on HIGH for 2 minutes or until melted.

Beat in the water, lime juice, and egg yolks. Cook on MEDIUM for 1 minute; whisk well. (Immediately after cooking, the sauce will appear curdled, but after beating, it will smooth out.) Cook on MEDIUM for 30 seconds more or until thick. (It will thicken more upon cooling, too.)

Beat in the lime rind and cayenne.

Serve in a bowl, hollowed out acorn squash, or lettuce cup, surrounded by the vegetables.

FISH FILLETS IN SPINACH NESTS WITH FRESH TOMATO-TARRAGON COULIS

The spinach nests cradle the fish fillets while the chopped tomato sauce surrounds them in a contrasting rosy pool.

On a 12-inch round microwaveproof platter, place the garlic and butter. Cover with plastic wrap turned back slightly on one side, and cook on HIGH for 1 minute or until the butter is melted. Pile the spinach over the melted butter (it will be a high pile). Cover again and cook on HIGH for 2 minutes. Stir well to coat the spinach leaves with the butter-garlic mixture. Sprinkle with the nutmeg, salt, and pepper. Push the leaves into 4 mounds, leaving the center of the dish open.

Fold the thinner ends of each fish fillet under the thicker center in a two-fold-letter fashion. Place them seam side down, one on top of each spinach nest. Sprinkle with the lemon juice. Cover with wax paper. Cook on HIGH for 8 to 10 minutes or until the fish flakes under the pressure of a fork. Let stand, covered, while making the coulis.

To make the coulis, place the garlic, onions, and 1 tablespoon of the butter into a 4-cup glass measure. Cook on HIGH for 1 minute. Add the tomatoes, tarragon leaves, vinegar, cream, and pepper. Cook on HIGH for 2 to 3 minutes, until heated through, stirring once. Stir in the remaining 2 tablespoons butter until melted.

To serve, place 1 nest on each dinner plate, with a spatula. Spoon 1 tablespoon coulis on the side of each nest. Spoon a ribbon of coulis down the center of the fish. Garnish with a lemon wedge and a tarragon sprig.

Serves: 4

Cooking time: 14 to 16 minutes

1 garlic clove, minced
2 tablespoons unsalted butter
1 pound spinach leaves, washed and drained well, with stems removed and leaves cut into 1-inch ribbons
¼ teaspoon freshly grated nutmeg
¼ teaspoon salt
¼ teaspoon freshly ground black pepper
4 thin fish fillets (flounder or sole) (about 1 pound)
1 teaspoon lemon juice

COULIS:

1 garlic clove, minced
2 green onions, thinly sliced
3 tablespoons unsalted butter
1 cup peeled, seeded, and coarsely chopped plum tomatoes (about 1 pound) or 1 cup canned Italian plum tomatoes, drained
1 teaspoon chopped fresh tarragon leaves
1 teaspoon balsamic vinegar
1 tablespoon heavy cream
⅛ teaspoon freshly ground black pepper
Lemon wedges, for garnish
Tarragon sprigs, for garnish

BARLEY PILAF WITH SUNFLOWER SEEDS AND RADICCHIO

Serves: 4

Cooking time: 14 to 20 minutes

1 tablespoon olive oil
1 tablespoon unsalted butter (optional)
1 onion, chopped
¼ cup shelled sunflower seeds
1 cup pearl barley
1¾ cups chicken broth
1 tablespoon lemon juice
¼ teaspoon freshly ground black pepper
¼ pound radicchio leaves, torn into
    2-inch pieces

A simple but tempting combination of al dente barley, crunchy sunflower seeds, and bittersweet red radicchio. The barley is wonderful with fish.

In a 3-quart microwaveproof casserole, combine the olive oil, butter if desired, onion, and sunflower seeds. Cook, uncovered, on HIGH for 3 to 4 minutes or until the onion is tender and the sunflower seeds are slightly toasted.

Stir in the barley, coating every grain. Add the broth, lemon juice, and pepper. Cover tightly and cook on HIGH for 4 to 6 minutes or until the liquid is boiling; then cook on MEDIUM for 7 to 10 minutes or until most of the liquid has been absorbed and the barley is tender. Cover again and let stand for 5 minutes. Fold in the radicchio right before serving.

Variations:

BASMATI PILAF WITH SUNFLOWER SEEDS AND RADICCHIO: Substitute 1 cup basmati rice for the barley and follow the basic recipe.

WILD RICE PILAF WITH SUNFLOWER SEEDS AND RADICCHIO: Substitute 1 cup wild rice for the barley, but increase the cooking time on MEDIUM to 20 to 25 minutes. This is especially nice with duck or other poultry.

POACHED FIGS WITH WHITE CHOCOLATE ANGLAISE

Serves: 4

Cooking time: 7 to 8 minutes

¼ cup dry white wine or water
2 tablespoons sugar
1 tablespoon orange-flavored liqueur (optional)
8 fresh figs
White Chocolate Anglaise (recipe follows)
Fresh mint, for garnish (optional)

In a casserole, combine the wine, sugar, and liqueur, stirring well. Add the figs. Cover tightly with the lid or plastic wrap turned back slightly on one side, and cook on HIGH for 2 minutes; turn the figs over and rearrange. Cover again and cook on HIGH for 1 to 3 minutes more or until the figs are tender. Cool, covered, in the cooking liquid, turning over once to coat.

To serve, spoon the anglaise onto flat dessert plates and place 2 figs on top of each plate. Drizzle more anglaise over top and garnish with mint, if desired.

Variation:

DARK CHOCOLATE ANGLAISE: Substitute dark chocolate for the white chocolate.

WHITE CHOCOLATE ANGLAISE

Makes: 1½ cups

Cooking time: 4 to 5 minutes

1 cup milk
1 ounce white chocolate
3 tablespoons sugar
3 egg yolks, lightly beaten
1 teaspoon vanilla extract, rum, or orange-flavored liqueur

Not as thick as a pastry cream, this sauce enhances poached fruit or cake.

Combine the milk, chocolate, and sugar in a 4-cup glass measure. Cook on HIGH for 3 to 4 minutes or until the chocolate is melted.

Slowly add the egg yolks in a steady stream to the chocolate mixture, whisking constantly. Cook on HIGH for 1 minute or until slightly thickened; whisk. If still not quite thick enough, cook on HIGH for 30 seconds more; beat. Stir in the vanilla. Cool the sauce with a piece of plastic wrap on the surface to keep a skin from forming. May be refrigerated for up to 2 days.

NORTHWEST EATING WITH A FRENCH TOUCH

Serves 8

Chilled Terrine with
Pistachios and Caper
Mustard

Rosemary Roast Chicken
and Roasted Garlic Cloves

Poultry Pan Drippings
Gravy

Hot 'n' Sour Sautéed
Cabbage and Apples

Couscous or Orzo

Crusty French Bread

Cranberry Trifle

Serves 8

Chilled Terrine with
Pistachios and Caper
Mustard

Rosemary Roast Chicken
and Roasted Garlic Cloves

Poultry Pan Drippings
Gravy

Hot 'n' Sour Sautéed
Cabbage and Apples

Couscous or Orzo

Crusty French Bread

Cranberry Trifle

WINE SUGGESTION
Northwest Sauvignon Blanc

NORTHWEST EATING WITH A FRENCH TOUCH

Wenatchee is a central Washington town that is abundant in its natural food resources, especially apples and other fruits. For a town of 40,000, it has ways of charming its guests with real European style. We enjoyed a lovely meal at a restaurant situated between mountains; the setting could just as well have been a village in southern France. We began with appetizers on a grape-arbored patio and the strains of a harpist. We moved inside and by the time we re-emerged, the stars had blanketed the sky and we were satiated with good food and drink. ¶ The following menu, with its chicken redolent of rosemary and garlic, reminds us of that wonderful night. The garlic is cooked right along with the chicken in the juices, and those juices added to chicken broth make an unforgettable sauce. The softened garlic can then be squeezed onto toasted French bread.

PREPARATION PLAN

UP TO 2 DAYS IN ADVANCE:

1. Prepare the trifle (up to final garnish of your choice) and terrine and refrigerate.
2. Make garnish, either orange strips (which are refrigerated in a sealed container), or chocolate leaves and berries.

2 HOURS BEFORE SERVING:

1. Prepare and cook the chicken.
2. Meanwhile, prepare the garlic.
3. During the second half of the cooking, prepare the ingredients for the cabbage and apples, and arrange plates for the terrine.
4. While the chicken is browning in the conventional oven, cook the cabbage in the microwave oven.
5. Cook couscous or orzo following package instructions on top of stove.
6. While the chicken and cabbage are standing, cook the gravy.

AT THE TABLE:

1. Serve the terrine.
2. Slice the chicken for serving, and reheat the cabbage on HIGH for 2 minutes and the gravy on HIGH for 1 minute, stirring before serving.
3. Whip cream for dessert; garnish and serve.

EVEN EASIER HINTS

1. Substitute Mixed Greens Salad with Pecan Vinaigrette (page 195) for the terrine.
2. Serve only the Hint-of-Orange Custard accompanied with fresh fruit. Orange slices, pineapple cubes, pears, any berry, or a fresh applesauce are excellent choices. Serve the custard warm if you like (it's delicious) and prepare it right before serving.

CHRISTMAS DINNER VARIATION: *With a few minor changes this menu can be turned into a Christmas dinner. Serve the couscous with ½ cup thinly sliced green onion tops folded in and substitute the Holiday Vegetable Platter (see page 134) for the Hot 'n' Sour Sautéed Cabbage and Apples. Add the Pine Nut Almond Cake (see page 302) and/or a good-quality vanilla ice cream topped with crushed peppermint candy and serve Christmas cookies.*

❡ Decorate rosemary topiary trees with tiny ornaments and ribbons. Give them to guests when they leave.

CHILLED TERRINE WITH PISTACHIOS AND CAPER MUSTARD

Serves: 8

Cooking time: 15 to 18 minutes

¼ cup finely chopped green onions
½ pound lean pork, ground from chunks
½ pound veal or turkey, ground
½ pound lean ham, cut into ½-inch cubes
4 egg whites, slightly beaten
¼ cup shelled pistachios
2 tablespoons cognac, vermouth, or
    sherry
¼ teaspoon ground allspice
¼ teaspoon freshly grated nutmeg
¼ teaspoon crushed thyme

GARNISHES:
1 bunch watercress
16 cornichons or small pickles
2 large carrots, peeled
½ cup Caper Mustard (recipe follows)

Made with turkey and pork (the other light meat) this dense "meatloaf" is lightly scented with cognac. Weighting the terrine will make a more solid mass for easier slicing. Keeping it refrigerated overnight will improve the flavor.

Combine all the ingredients, except the garnishes, and mix well. Press evenly into a loaf dish (9 × 5 inches). Cover loosely with wax paper and cook on HIGH for 15 to 18 minutes, until cooked through (the loaf should shrink slightly from the sides; the top should be firm to the touch with the juices running clear yellow, with no trace of pink).

Remove the wax paper, leaving the terrine in the dish. Cover the top with foil. Place a 1-pound weight on top of the foil and cool to room temperature. Refrigerate the weighted terrine overnight.

To serve, cut the loaf into 16 slices. Place 2 pieces of terrine on eight serving plates. Place a few sprigs of watercress on each plate at the base of the terrine, along with 2 cornichons. Cut the carrots into 3-inch sections; make thin, wide lengthwise slices with a vegetable peeler. Add as a garnish with the watercress. Spoon 1 tablespoon of Caper Mustard onto each plate.

CAPER MUSTARD

Makes: 1 cup

1 cup coarse-grained Dijon mustard
2 tablespoons capers

Combine the ingredients in a small bowl.

ROSEMARY ROAST CHICKEN AND ROASTED GARLIC CLOVES

For a smaller 2- to 6-pound chicken, cook on HIGH 6 to 9 minutes per pound.

Rub the chicken with the lemon quarters. Place the lemon quarters into the cavity along with 2 sprigs of the rosemary. Lightly salt and pepper the bird.

Truss the bird by tying the legs together and the wings to the body. Place, breast side down, in a 3-quart rectangular microwaveproof dish. Cook in the microwave oven, uncovered, on HIGH for 10 minutes, then on MEDIUM for 35 minutes.

Turn the bird over. Add the garlic cloves to the cooking dish. Cook on MEDIUM for 30 to 35 minutes or until the juices run clear when pierced between the thickest part of the leg and body.

Meanwhile, preheat the conventional oven to 500°F. Transfer the dish with the chicken and garlic to the preheated oven for 5 to 10 minutes to crisp (watch the time carefully). Remove the chicken and let it stand, covered loosely with foil, for 10 minutes before serving. Make the gravy during the standing time.

To serve, garnish a serving platter with the lemon slices and the remaining rosemary sprigs.

NOTE: If all the garlic hasn't softened by the time the chicken is finished, transfer the chicken to the platter to stand, and continue cooking the garlic in the pan juices in the microwave oven for 5 minutes more on MEDIUM or until soft.

Serves: 8

Cooking time: 1 hour 30 minutes

1 (8-pound) roasting chicken
2 lemons (1 quartered and 1 thinly sliced for garnish)
10 sprigs rosemary
Salt and freshly ground black pepper
25 unmarked, perfect large garlic cloves, separated but unpeeled (about 2 large heads)

POULTRY PAN DRIPPINGS GRAVY

Makes: About 1 cup

Cooking time: 5 to 8 minutes

2 tablespoons fat from drippings
1½ tablespoons all-purpose flour
1 cup chicken broth or a combination of broth and defatted pan juices
1 tablespoon dry vermouth
Salt and freshly ground black pepper to taste

This recipe can yield quick gravy for turkey or turkey breast, chicken, or game hens.

Combine the fat and flour in a 4-cup glass measure. Stir in the broth and vermouth until smooth. Cook on HIGH for 5 to 8 minutes or until thickened, stirring 2 to 3 times with a wire whisk to keep smooth. Salt and pepper to taste.

ROSEMARY *This herb comes from a small evergreen shrub of the mint family. In some homes on the Mediterranean, an area where rosemary is native, it is often planted by the front door or placed in pots in the home to give off a wonderful pine scent. The flavoring in foods is just as clean and clear with a hint of pine needles in it.*
❦ *One legend says that rosemary will grow only in the garden of the righteous; thank heavens then for produce markets where it can be purchased for cooking with lamb, poultry, seafood, tomato sauces for pasta, breads, and even thrown over hot coals for barbecuing.* ❦ *You can carry out the theme of this meal by tying a sprig of rosemary to the rolled napkins that you place on the table.*

HOT 'N' SOUR SAUTÉED CABBAGE AND APPLES

Combine the butter and onions in a 3-quart micro-waveproof casserole. Cook on HIGH for 1 minute to melt the butter. Add the cabbage and apples. Cover tightly and cook on HIGH for 5 to 7 minutes or until tender-crisp; stir well. Let stand, covered, while cooking the sauce.

Meanwhile, in a 1-cup glass measure, combine the vinegar, brown sugar, and cornstarch. Cook on HIGH for 1 to 2 minutes or until slightly thickened, stirring once. Stir into the cabbage with the raisins. Re-cover the cabbage and set aside.

Serves: 8

Cooking time: 7 to 10 minutes

2 tablespoons unsalted butter
¼ cup thinly sliced green onions
2 pounds savoy cabbage, sliced into
    ¼-inch strips
2 tart apples (Granny Smith), cored, but
    not peeled, and thinly sliced
2 tablespoons balsamic vinegar
¼ cup brown sugar
1 teaspoon cornstarch
½ cup golden raisins

HOLIDAY VEGETABLE PLATTER

Serves: 10 to 12

Cooking time: 5 to 8 minutes

1 medium-size acorn squash, halved, seeded, unpeeled, and cut into ¼-inch crosswise slices
Broccoli flowerets from 1 head of broccoli (about 2 cups)
3 large carrots, cut into 2-inch-by-¼-inch strips (about 1½ cups)
2 cups mushroom caps
1 red bell pepper, seeded and cut into ½-inch lengthwise strips
2 tablespoons water

This attractive vegetable platter makes an edible centerpiece. The variety of vegetables will appeal to most tastes. A Fresh Lemon Herb Sauce (recipe follows) enhances the vegetables, but they are delicious on their own.

Around the outside rim of a 12- to 14-inch circular microwaveproof platter, arrange acorn squash slices slightly overlapping to form an edible doily.

Arrange broccoli flowerets next to squash with the stalks facing toward the outer rim.

Arrange carrots against the broccoli and place mushroom caps in the center.

Arrange the red pepper strips on top of the vegetables in a spoke fashion, points meeting in the center of the dish, to form a poinsettia-like blossom.

Sprinkle with water. Cover with plastic wrap, turning up one corner to vent. Cook on HIGH for 5 to 8 minutes, or until tender-crisp.

FRESH LEMON HERB SAUCE

Makes: 1 cup

Cooking time: 1 minute

½ cup unsalted butter
2 tablespoons finely chopped fresh parsley
2 tablespoons finely chopped fresh dill
2 tablespoons finely chopped chives
2 tablespoons fresh lemon juice

Place butter into a 2-cup glass measure and cook on HIGH for 1 to 2 minutes, until melted. Stir in remaining ingredients. Pour into a serving bowl. Serve with vegetable platter.

CRANBERRY TRIFLE

Cranberries sparkle through the custard like garnets in snow. Glazed cranberries and chocolate leaves (recipes follow) will add a festive touch to the trifle (or any holiday cake, for that matter). Decorate the top with a ring of leaves in pairs with clusters of cranberries.

Cut the cake into 1-inch cubes. Line the bottom of a 2-quart crystal bowl or trifle dish with ⅓ of the cubes. Sprinkle with 1 tablespoon of the orange liqueur. Spoon ⅓ of the cranberry sauce evenly over the cubes. Pour ⅓ of the custard over the cubes.

Repeat two more times; cover and refrigerate overnight.

Before serving, whip the cream with the vanilla. Spoon over the trifle and garnish with strips of orange rind that have been rolled into loose corkscrews.

Serves: 8

Cooking time: 9 to 13 minutes

1 (10¾-ounce) frozen pound cake
3 tablespoons orange-flavored liqueur
2 cups Cranberry Sauce (recipe follows)
2 cups Hint-of-Orange Custard (recipe follows)
1 cup heavy cream
1 teaspoon vanilla extract
8 to 10 long strips of orange rind

CRANBERRY SAUCE

When you are not making the trifle for dessert, this sauce can be served along with any roast poultry. A wax paper cover will prevent spatters without causing a boilover the way a tight cover would.

Combine all the ingredients in a 2-quart microwave-proof casserole. Cover with wax paper and cook on HIGH for 4 to 6 minutes or until the berries have popped, stirring after 2 minutes. Cool.

Makes: About 2 cups

Cooking time: 4 to 6 minutes

12 ounces fresh or 1 (2-ounce) package frozen unsweetened cranberries
1 cup sugar
¼ cup orange-flavored liqueur or orange juice

HINT-OF-ORANGE CUSTARD

Makes: About 2 cups

Cooking time: 5 to 7 minutes

2 cups milk
¼ cup sugar
4 egg yolks
2 tablespoons all-purpose flour
2 tablespoons grated orange rind
1 tablespoon orange-flavored liqueur

Pour the milk into a 4-cup glass measure. Cook on HIGH for 3 minutes or until hot but not boiling.

Meanwhile, in a 2-quart microwaveproof casserole, beat the sugar into the egg yolks until blended. Stir in the flour. Gradually add the heated milk, beating constantly. Cook on HIGH for 1 minute; beat with a whisk. Cook on HIGH for 1 to 3 minutes more or until the mixture coats a spoon, beating every 30 seconds. Stir in the orange rind and liqueur; cool.

Variation:

TRADITIONAL TRIFLE WITH BERRIES: Substitute 2 cups sliced strawberries for the Cranberry Sauce. Garnish the top with whole strawberries.

SUGAR-GLAZED CRANBERRIES

Makes: 24 cranberries

Cooking time: 5 to 6 minutes

½ cup sugar
2 tablespoons water
24 fresh cranberries, washed and dried well
24 toothpicks

Line a cookie sheet with wax paper.

In a 4-cup glass measure, combine the sugar and water; mix well to dissolve the sugar. Cook on HIGH for 2 minutes; stir gently to redistribute the heat. Cook on HIGH for 3 to 4 minutes more, or until the syrup is amber colored and a spoonful becomes brittle when dropped into ice water.

Meanwhile, skewer the cranberries with the toothpicks. When the syrup is ready, stir it once or twice, gently.

Working quickly, dip a few berries into the syrup to

coat, and remove individually onto the cookie sheet and remove toothpicks. They will begin to harden immediately.

When hardened, pack in a single layer into an airtight container. Refrigerate until ready to use. Packaged in this way, they may be stored for 3 days.

NOTE: Orange segments or strawberries (24 small) may be substituted for the cranberries; use a fork rather than toothpicks to handle.

CHOCOLATE HOLLY LEAVES

Makes: 18

Cooking time: 2½ to 3 minutes

6 ounces semisweet chocolate pieces
18 fabric holly leaves or lemon leaves, washed and dried (see Note)

Line a cookie sheet with wax paper; set aside.

Arrange the chocolate pieces in a circle around the outer rim of a microwaveproof cereal bowl, leaving the center free (or use a paper bowl and throw it away). Cook on MEDIUM for 2½ to 3 minutes or until the chocolate is just soft enough to spread, stirring after 2 minutes and then checking every 30 seconds thereafter.

When the chocolate is softened, and working quickly, use a pastry brush to paint the chocolate on the outside of the leaves, spreading the chocolate as evenly as possible, about ⅛ inch thick (if it is too thin, it will break upon hardening). Place the leaves on the cookie sheet.

Freeze the chocolate until hardened. When hardened, carefully pull the chocolate from the leaves and spread out in a container for storage, using wax paper between the layers. Freeze until ready to use.

NOTE: Since real holly leaves are poisonous we suggest using fabric (not plastic) that can be purchased at minimal cost and may be reused many times.

MOGUL DINNER

Serves 8

Spiced Nuts Under Glass

Irresistible Spiced Popcorn

Fried Carrot and Potato
Patties with Minted
Cucumber Raita

Chicken Curry with Golden
Raisins

Fragrant Basmati Rice

Pineapple Chutney

Warmed Pitas or
Pappadams

Mango Cream

Spiced Tea with Warm Milk

MOGUL DINNER

Serves 8

Spiced Nuts Under Glass

Irresistible Spiced Popcorn

Fried Carrot and Potato
Patties with Minted
Cucumber Raita

Chicken Curry with Golden
Raisins

Fragrant Basmati Rice

Pineapple Chutney

Warmed Pitas or
Pappadams

Mango Cream

Spiced Tea with Warm Milk

BEVERAGE SUGGESTION
Indian beer, if available, or
other imported beer
or Sauvignon Blanc

Something about Indian meals makes them fun for a group. Perhaps it is the fact that the parts of the meal that are terrifically spicy will excite the palate as well as conversation, for there is always someone in the crowd who knows best how to quench the flame (bread or yogurt works; water —never; and beer is worth a try!). ❡ The hot tea is regularly served with warm milk and sugar, all mixed together according to the taste of the host. Although we usually don't take either coffee or tea with sugar and milk, it seems essential to an Indian meal. A train trip across India is not complete without thermoses of the stuff delivered to your seat, perhaps to lubricate thought or conversation. We hope you will enjoy lingering long over a cup or two with your guests. ❡ Sprinkle candied rose petals on top of the Mango Cream for a nice touch.

PREPARATION PLAN

THE DAY BEFORE:
1. Cook the chicken curry (this may be done 2 days in advance) and refrigerate.
2. Make the nuts (see page 111).
3. Make the raita and refrigerate.
4. Make the chutney and refrigerate.
5. Cut up the mangoes and freeze.

2 HOURS BEFORE SERVING:
1. Slice, chop, and assemble the ingredients for the fried vegetable patties.
2. Pop the corn.
3. Chop ¼ cup cilantro and slice 2 limes for curry.

1 HOUR BEFORE SERVING:
1. Cook the rice; then let it stand until serving time.
2. Add spices to corn and set out.
3. Meanwhile, prepare the Mango Cream; refreeze.
4. As guests arrive, put out the nuts (in glass jars or in bowls) and popcorn.
5. After cooking the rice, reheat the curry.
6. Press out any liquid that may have drained from the grated vegetables. Combine the vegetables with the remaining ingredients. Fry the patties and let them stand on paper towels until serving.

AT THE TABLE:
1. Serve the patties as a first course, with the raita, or serve all together as a buffet with the curry, rice, and breads.
2. If serving separate courses, clear the table and heat the pitas or pappadams.
3. Serve the chicken, rice, chutney, and breads.
4. Afterwards, prepare the hot tea and serve the Mango Cream.

EVEN EASIER HINTS
1. Substitute Mango Slices and Ice Cream (see page 149) for the Mango Cream.
2. Instead of the Mango Cream, serve ½ gallon of a good-quality vanilla ice cream sprinkled with nutmeg and ½ cup chopped pistachio nuts.

IRRESISTIBLE SPICED POPCORN

Makes: 2 cups

Cooking time: 3 minutes

⅓ cup popcorn
2 tablespoons unsalted butter or
    margarine
1 to 2 teaspoons chili powder
Pinch ground cinnamon

Our friend Susan Cioni serves this often at her catered dinners for others. It does require at least a 650-watt microwave oven to pop the corn well.

Place the popcorn in a brown sandwich-size bag. Gently fold down the top of the bag twice to close lightly but firmly. Cook on HIGH for 2½ to 3 minutes or until the popping begins to slow down but is not completely stopped, watching closely during the last minute. Remove and set aside.

Place the butter in a 1-cup glass measure. Cook on HIGH for 35 to 45 seconds or until melted. Stir in the chili and cinnamon. Pour the popcorn into a serving bowl. Drizzle the butter mixture on top and stir until well coated. Serve.

Variation:

CAJUN POPCORN: Substitute 3 to 4 drops Tabasco for the chili powder and ⅛ teaspoon cayenne pepper for the cinnamon.

NOTE: To double the recipe, repeat the procedure rather than cooking double the amount at one time.

FRIED CARROT AND POTATO PATTIES WITH MINTED CUCUMBER RAITA

The raita is often served as a type of salad or side dish, but it is creamy enough to be a cooling dipping sauce for these crispy patties.

Combine all the ingredients for the raita in a small bowl; chill.

To make the patties, combine the vegetables and flour in a medium bowl, toss to coat the vegetables well. Add the remaining ingredients except the peanut oil and mint leaves.

Pour peanut oil, ¼ inch deep, into a large, heavy skillet and heat until hot but not smoking. Drop rounded tablespoonfuls of the vegetable mixture into the oil and flatten to form disks; there should be about 8 in the first batch. Brown well on one side, about 1 minute. (It is important to brown well before turning over, to keep them from falling apart.) Turn over and brown the other side. Drain on paper towels. Repeat the process with the second batch.

To serve, place 2 patties on each plate along with 2 tablespoons of the raita; garnish with mint leaves.

NOTE: If making earlier in the day, don't refrigerate or the patties will turn soggy; instead, keep them at room temperature.

To reheat, line two 12-inch plates with paper towels and place 8 patties around the outer edge of the plate. Cover with paper towels. Heat one plate at a time on HIGH for 1 minute. While one plate is heating, spoon 1 tablespoon of the raita on each of eight small individual appetizer plates. Place 2 hot patties on each plate, and repeat the reheating process. Garnish with mint.

Makes: 16 patties with 2 cups sauce

Cooking time: 5 minutes

RAITA:

1 cucumber, peeled, seeded and grated (about 1 cup)
1 cup plain yogurt
1 tablespoon chopped fresh mint
½ teaspoon ground cumin
Dash cayenne pepper

VEGETABLE PATTIES:

3 large carrots, peeled and grated (1½ cups)
2 medium-size Idaho or russet potatoes, peeled and grated (½ cup)
4 green onions, thinly sliced
2 tablespoons all-purpose flour
1 egg, beaten
¼ teaspoon freshly ground black pepper
¼ teaspoon salt
Dash cayenne pepper
Peanut oil, for frying
Mint leaves, for garnish

CHICKEN CURRY WITH GOLDEN RAISINS

Serves: 8

Cooking time: About 30 minutes

3 cups chicken broth

2 tablespoons peanut or vegetable oil

2 garlic cloves, minced

2 cups chopped onions

1 cup finely sliced celery

3 tablespoons curry powder

¼ cup all-purpose flour

2 pounds boneless chicken breasts, cut into 1-inch cubes

1 cup golden raisins

GARNISH:

2 limes, cut into 16 wedges

¼ cup chopped fresh coriander (cilantro)

1 cup roasted unsalted peanuts, coarsely chopped

Heating the broth alone first speeds the cooking process later, and gives you time to chop the other ingredients.

Pour the chicken broth into a 4-cup glass measure. Heat on HIGH for 6 to 7 minutes. Set aside.

In a 3-quart microwaveproof casserole, combine the oil, garlic, onion, celery, and curry powder. Stir well to mix. Cover tightly with the lid or plastic wrap turned back slightly on one side, and cook on HIGH for 5 to 7 minutes or until the vegetables are tender-crisp, stirring halfway through the cooking.

Stir in the flour until it is blended. Slowly stir in the broth. Cover again and cook on HIGH for 6 to 8 minutes or until it has begun to boil and thicken, stirring once. Add the chicken and raisins; stir well. Re-cover and cook on HIGH for 10 to 12 minutes or until the chicken is cooked through, stirring once. Let stand, covered, for 10 minutes.

Serve curry on individual dishes over rice with the 2 wedges of lime; sprinkle on top with the chopped coriander and peanuts.

NOTE: To reheat refrigerated curry, heat covered with the lid or plastic wrap turned back slightly on one side on HIGH for 5 minutes; stir. Re-cover and cook on MEDIUM for 15 to 20 minutes, stirring twice, until heated through. (As you can see, this time is almost as much as for cooking, but you do save the chopping time.)

CURRY POWDER

Curry powder, an amalgam of spices, is readily available as a packaged product, yet a true Indian cook would never use the same standard "curry" for all dishes. If you feel inclined to give this chicken dish a special stamp, here is a recipe for a curry blend that makes 3 tablespoons. To make your own favorite powder, experiment with varying amounts of each spice.

Combine all the ingredients in a small bowl and blend well.

Makes: 3 tablespoons

2 teaspoons ground coriander
2 teaspoons ground cumin
1 teaspoon turmeric
1 teaspoon ground cinnamon
1 teaspoon dried oregano leaves
1 teaspoon ground ginger
1 teaspoon freshly ground black pepper
½ teaspoon cayenne pepper
½ teaspoon ground nutmeg
¼ teaspoon ground cloves

FRAGRANT BASMATI RICE

Serves: 8

Cooking time: About 20 minutes

3½ cups water

2 cups basmati rice

2 cups fresh or 1 (10-ounce) package frozen peas

4 sticks cinnamon, broken in half

½ teaspoon salt (optional)

This colorful and aromatic rice dish is especially complementary to spicy dishes.

Combine all the ingredients in a 3-quart microwave-proof casserole. Cover tightly with the lid or plastic wrap turned back slightly on one side. Cook on HIGH for 8 to 10 minutes or until boiling; then cook on MEDIUM for 10 to 12 minutes or until most of the water is absorbed and the rice is tender. Let stand, covered, for at least 5 minutes.

BASMATI RICE *This is a long-grain rice that is grown in the northern part of India and Pakistan. It has a low proportion of waxy starch, which causes it to be dry and flaky when cooked. It is generally converted before milling, which means that the B vitamins are allowed to permeate the rice kernel before the bran is removed.* ❦ *Look at the rice before cooking. Sometimes but not always it may need a quick rinse to remove little stones. The aroma and flavor of this rice as it cooks hints at the fragrant scents found in the Indian bazaar—it's wonderful!*

PINEAPPLE CHUTNEY

This chutney is a wonderful condiment for this meal. We always hope that there will be some left over to spoon over frozen yogurt for a special treat.

Remove the peel and core from the fresh pineapple and cut into ½-inch chunks.

Place the pineapple and brown sugar into a 2-quart microwaveproof casserole, cover tightly with the lid or plastic wrap turned back slightly on one side, and cook on HIGH for 3 minutes. Meanwhile, combine the cornstarch and vinegar in a small bowl until smooth. Stir into the pineapple. Add the remaining ingredients. Cover again and cook on HIGH for 8 to 10 minutes, stirring after 4 minutes. Set aside or chill. Serve at room temperature or chilled.

Makes: 3 cups

Cooking time: 11 to 13 minutes

1 firm ripe pineapple (about 3 pounds) or
    4 cups drained, unsweetened chunks
½ cup dark brown sugar
1 teaspoon cornstarch
¼ cup cider vinegar
1 tablespoon finely grated fresh ginger
½ teaspoon salt
½ teaspoon dry mustard
1 jalapeño pepper, seeded and finely
    chopped (less if you don't like it hot)

WARMED PITAS AND PAPPADAMS *To heat pitas, wrap 8 in a paper towel and heat on HIGH for 1 minute.* ¶ *Pappadams are spicy, thin, round biscuits made of lentil powder. They can be baked or fried, and heat up beautifully in the microwave oven when wrapped in paper towels. You can purchase them in specialty or Indian stores; they will have microwave instructions right on them.*

MANGO CREAM

Serves: 8

Cooking time: 1 to 2 minutes

3 ripe mangoes (about 1 pound each)
3 tablespoons sugar
½ cup plain yogurt
2 tablespoons orange-flavored liqueur or
    orange juice
1 teaspoon vanilla extract
Fresh mint leaves, for garnish

Perfectly ripened mangoes will make the difference in this delicious and refreshing dessert. You can see that this recipe is easy to cut in half, something which we often do for family meals, as it is a favorite.

Peel the mangoes and remove the seeds. Cut the mangoes into 1-inch cubes and place them on a cookie sheet. Freeze for 1 hour or until partially frozen.

Place half of the frozen mango cubes in the bowl of a food processor. Add 1½ tablespoons of the sugar, ¼ cup of the yogurt, 1 tablespoon of the liqueur, and ½ teaspoon of the vanilla. Process until smooth. Follow the same procedure with the remaining ingredients. You may serve the cream at this point or spoon it into a container and freeze for 1 to 2 hours.

If serving immediately, spoon into long-stemmed glasses and garnish with mint leaves. If freezing, serve with a scoop, as you would a sorbet, also into long-stemmed glasses, and garnish with mint.

NOTE: To slightly defrost the Mango Cream for scooping, remove the lid from the container and heat in the microwave oven on DEFROST for 2 to 3 minutes.

If you have frozen the mango cubes for too long, defrost them in two batches. Place the first batch of frozen cubes in a microwaveproof bowl. Heat on DEFROST for 1 minute. Follow the same procedure with the second batch. If freeze is too hard to scoop, heat on DEFROST for 2 to 3 minutes.

MANGO SLICES AND ICE CREAM

Serves: 8

Here's an even easier dessert when time is short.

Divide the mango slices among eight dessert plates and fan them out. Place a scoop of ice cream at the base of each fan and top with a sprinkling of nutmeg.

3 ripe mangoes (1 pound each), peeled and cut into long, thin slices
½ gallon good-quality vanilla ice cream
Freshly grated nutmeg

SPICED TEA WITH WARM MILK

Makes: 10 6-ounce cups

Cooking time: 16 to 20 minutes

Water boils almost as efficiently on top of the stove as it does in the microwave oven. The advantage of using the microwave oven is that you can measure and then heat the water in an 8-cup glass measure and you don't need to "watch the pot" while entertaining.

Place cloves and cinnamon into a small piece of cheesecloth and tie securely with kitchen string. If using loose tea follow the same procedure.

Pour water into an 8-cup glass measure, cover with vented plastic wrap, and cook on HIGH for 15 to 18 minutes, until boiling. Add spice bag, lemon and orange peel, and tea to boiling water. Allow to steep for 5 minutes. Remove tea and spices and pour into a serving container.

To warm milk, pour 1 cup of milk into a 1-cup glass measure. Heat on HIGH for 1 to 2 minutes until warm but not boiling. Pour into a serving pitcher. Serve tea along with milk and sugar to taste.

6 whole cloves
1 3-inch stick cinnamon, broken in half
8 cups water
2 pieces lemon peel, 2 inches long by ½ inch wide
2 pieces orange peel, 2 inches long by ½ inch wide
3 tablespoons loose black tea or 7 (orange pekoe) tea bags
1 cup milk
Sugar

BLACK TIE AND TAILS DINNER

Serves 4

Champagne-Steamed
Mussels with Basil or
Cilantro Mayonnaise

or

Steamed Artichokes with
Basil or Cilantro
Mayonnaise

Chicken Breasts and
Zucchini Wrapped in
Romaine Leaves

Coucous-and-Scallion
Timbales with Lemon

Onion Marmalade

Lemon Mousse

BLACK TIE AND TAILS DINNER

Champagne-Steamed
Mussels with Basil or
Cilantro Mayonnaise

or

Steamed Artichokes with
Basil or Cilantro
Mayonnaise

Chicken Breasts and
Zucchini Wrapped in
Romaine Leaves

Couscous-and-Scallion
Timbales with Lemon

Onion Marmalade

Lemon Mousse

WINE SUGGESTION
Champagne or Mâcon Blanc

T his would be a wonderful dinner served after the theater or to celebrate some special event. The first course calls for champagne with the mussels or Mâcon Blanc with the artichokes; the lemon mousse is fresh and tangy garnished with edible flowers—the perfect ending for this delightful meal. ¶ This is one of those meals that can be almost fully prepared in advance, with just a half-hour's preparation when you get home. You could even serve the chilled first course immediately, while the couscous is heating; the chicken could then quickly be cooked while you clear the table.

PREPARATION PLAN

EARLIER IN THE DAY OR THE DAY BEFORE:

1. Cook the mussels or artichokes and refrigerate.
2. Make the mayonnaise and refrigerate.
3. Make the Onion Marmalade and refrigerate.
4. Prepare and freeze the Lemon Mousse.

2 HOURS BEFORE SERVING:

1. Prepare and roll the chicken; chill.
2. Make scallion brushes for couscous.

½ HOUR BEFORE SERVING:

1. Remove the first course, mayonnaise, and marmalade from the refrigerator if you plan to serve them at room temperature.
2. Cook the couscous.
3. Cook the chicken.
4. While the chicken is cooking, spoon the couscous into timbale forms.

AT THE TABLE:

1. Serve the first course.
2. Make the sauce for the chicken and serve with the couscous timbales and marmalade.
3. Serve the dessert.

EVEN EASIER HINTS

1. Substitute Peppered Pink Pears (see page 61) for the Lemon Mousse.
2. Substitute a store-bought vegetable marmalade or chutney for the Onion Marmalade.

BASIL *Basil is one of the most savory of herbs and is a member of the mint family. Because of its delicate flavor, it may be used generously in a variety of vegetables, cheeses, and breads. ❡ Native to India, it was once worshiped there. An East Indian belief promises that the house surrounded by basil will be blessed. We like to believe this and grow abundant amounts of basil, which we use in pesto, soups, tomato salads, pasta sauces, ragouts, cheese mixtures, and with meats. ❡ Before the frost sets in, we remove the remaining leaves from our basil plants, wash and dry them well, and then freeze the leaves. The flavor is superior to dried leaves, which almost bear no relation to fresh basil.*

CHAMPAGNE-STEAMED MUSSELS WITH BASIL OR CILANTRO MAYONNAISE

Serves: 4

Cooking time: 7 to 9 minutes

1 medium-size onion, chopped
1 fennel bulb, thinly sliced (1 cup)
1 garlic clove, minced
1 tablespoon chopped parsley
½ cup champagne
2 pounds mussels, cleaned and scrubbed
Basil or Cilantro Mayonnaise (recipe
    follows)

Chilled champagne is the obvious libation to serve here and calls for a toast, so have one in mind.

Combine all the ingredients except the mussels and mayonnaise in a 3-quart microwaveproof casserole. Cook on HIGH for 3 minutes.

Add the mussels and cover with the lid or plastic wrap turned back slightly on one side. Cook on HIGH for 4 to 6 minutes or until the mussels are open, stirring after 3 minutes. Discard any unopened mussels and bring to room temperature. Chill in the poaching liquid for at least 1 hour.

Serve chilled in bowls, with the poaching liquid spooned on top. Place a small dish of the mayonnaise next to each plate along with lemon or lime wedges.

CLEANING MUSSELS

Cleaning mussels is a distasteful but necessary task if you want to avoid the gritty dirt that accompanies these delicious mollusks. Place the mussels in cold water as soon as you bring them home; if necessary, cover the bowl and keep refrigerated until the next day. To clean, discard any broken or slightly open shells. Remove any hard beard with a knife, and scrub and wash the shells in several changes of cold water. The last rinse should come out clean before the mussels are ready to use.

BASIL MAYONNAISE

Combine all the ingredients in a small bowl, and chill until serving time.

Variation:

CILANTRO MAYONNAISE: Substitute 1 tablespoon lime juice for the lemon juice and 1 cup chopped fresh cilantro for the basil.

Makes: 1½ cups

1 cup good-quality or Homemade Mayonnaise (recipe follows)
1 tablespoon lemon juice
1 cup chopped fresh basil

HOMEMADE MAYONNAISE

In the bowl of a food processor or blender, combine the egg, salt, and dry mustard; process to mix. Pour in the lemon juice and process quickly. As the processor is running, pour in the oil in a very slow, steady stream. As the oil is incorporated, the consistency will become thick and creamy.

Makes: 1 cup

1 large egg
¼ teaspoon salt
¼ teaspoon dry mustard
1 tablespoon lemon juice
1 cup oil (½ cup olive oil and ½ cup vegetable oil)

CHICKEN BREASTS AND ZUCCHINI WRAPPED IN ROMAINE LEAVES

Serves: 4

Cooking time: About 10 minutes

4 chicken breast halves (about 1 pound),
    boned and skinned
4 large romaine lettuce leaves
Salt
Freshly ground black pepper
⅛ teaspoon freshly ground nutmeg
2 small zucchini (about ½ pound), cut
    into 3- by ¼-inch strips
1 garlic clove, minced
2 tablespoons unsalted butter
¼ cup dry white wine
¾ cup light cream
2 tablespoons tomato paste
Dash cayenne pepper
Salt and freshly ground black pepper to
    taste

Place the chicken between two pieces of wax paper and flatten with a meat pounder to about ¼ inch. Set aside. Place the romaine leaves on a 10-inch round microwaveproof platter. Cover tightly with plastic wrap turned back slightly on one side, and cook on HIGH for 35 to 50 seconds to make them slightly pliable.

Place a chicken breast half on each leaf. Sprinkle lightly with salt, pepper, and the nutmeg. Divide the zucchini strips into 4 bunches and place at the top of the chicken breasts. Tuck any excess lettuce leaf over the sides of the chicken. Starting at the end with the zucchini, roll the lettuce and chicken in jelly-roll fashion (see illustration below).

Place the rolls seam side down in a circle on the 10-inch platter, leaving at least 1 inch between them. Place the garlic, butter, and wine in the center of the platter. Cover tightly again and cook on HIGH for 8 to 10 minutes or until the chicken is cooked through. Place a kitchen towel on top of the plastic wrap, and drain the cooking juices from the vented side into a 2-cup glass measure; there should be about ¼ cup. Let the chicken stand, covered, until serving time.

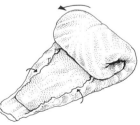
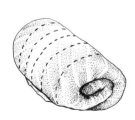

To the 2-cup measure with the cooking juices, add the cream, tomato paste, cayenne, salt, and black pepper. Cook on HIGH for 3 to 5 minutes or until bubbling and slightly thickened.

To serve, spoon 2 tablespoons of the sauce onto each plate. Cut each chicken roll into 6 crosswise pieces and arrange in a semicircle on the sauce. Spoon 2 tablespoons of the sauce over the chicken pieces.

Place a couscous timbale on each plate along with 2 tablespoons of Onion Marmalade (see page 159).

STEAMED ARTICHOKES WITH BASIL OR CILANTRO MAYONNAISE

This is an easy but elegant first course.

Serves: 4

Cooking time: 9 to 15 minutes

4 large artichokes (½ pound each)
1 lemon
Basil or Cilantro Mayonnaise (see page 155)

Cut off the artichoke stems, and trim about 1 inch from the top. Pull off the few small tough bottom leaves, and with scissors, snip off the tips of each of the outer leaves.

Cut the lemon in half crosswise and quarter one half; set the other half aside. Rub each artichoke with the cut side of a lemon quarter to prevent discoloration. Wrap each artichoke separately and tightly in plastic wrap. Place them on a microwaveproof plate, in a circle with at least 1-inch space between them. Cook on HIGH for 9 to 15 minutes or until tender and the base of each is easily pierced, rotating the dish one half-turn once. Chill the artichokes until serving time.

To serve, cut the remaining lemon half into 4 slices. Unwrap the artichokes and place each on an individual serving plate. Place a lemon slice on top of each artichoke. Serve each with a ramekin of ¼ cup mayonnaise.

COUSCOUS-AND-SCALLION TIMBALES WITH LEMON

Serves: 4

Cooking time: 3 to 5 minutes

6 scallions
1 cup dry couscous
1 tablespoon unsalted butter
1½ cups chicken broth
4 lemon slices, for garnish

Thinly slice 2 scallions, both the white and green parts; make scallion brushes of the remaining 4 scallions and set them aside.

In a 4-cup glass measure, combine the couscous, sliced scallions, butter, and broth. Cover tightly with the lid or plastic wrap turned back slightly on one side, and cook on HIGH for 3 to 5 minutes or until the mixture reaches a rapid boil. Stir well and let stand for 5 minutes.

Spoon the mixture into four 5- or 6-ounce custard cups or ramekins, patting down to make compact timbales. Cover and set aside until serving time.

To serve, run a knife around the edges of the custard cups and invert onto the dinner plates. Garnish the top of each timbale with a lemon slice, placing a scallion brush beside.

Variation:

COUSCOUS-AND-CHIVE TIMBALES FOR TWO: Eliminate the scallions and lemon slices.

In a 4-cup glass measure, combine ½ cup couscous, ¾ cup chicken broth, and 1 tablespoon lemon juice. Cover tightly and cook on HIGH for 5 minutes or until the mixture has boiled and all the liquid is absorbed. Fold in 2 tablespoons chopped chives. Mold as directed above. Turn out onto the serving plates and garnish with an X of chive blades.

NOTE: If you wish to prepare couscous in advance, cook and spoon into timbales. Place on a 10- or 12-inch microwaveproof dish and heat on HIGH for 2 to 4 minutes until top is warm to the touch. Turn out onto serving dishes.

ONION MARMALADE

These caramelized onions are delicious with any meat or poultry.

Combine the butter and onions in a 2-quart micro-waveproof casserole. Cook on HIGH for 5 minutes, stirring once. Stir in the brown sugar, vinegar, and thyme. Cook on HIGH for 5 minutes more. Let stand for 5 minutes. Serve warm, at room temperature, or chilled.

Makes: 2 cups

Cooking time: 10 minutes

2 tablespoons unsalted butter or
    margarine
1 pound red onions, peeled and cut into
    ½-inch cubes
1 tablespoon brown sugar
1 tablespoon balsamic vinegar
¼ teaspoon thyme

TO MAKE A SCALLION BRUSH *Trim the green from 4 scallions. Slice down from the cut end to the base about halfway, all the way around to make a fringed end. Place in ice water until ready to serve. The ends will curl slightly.*

LEMON MOUSSE

Serves: 4

Cooking time: 3 to 4 minutes

⅓ cup strained fresh lemon juice

1 teaspoon grated lemon rind

2 large eggs, separated

¾ cup granulated sugar

⅛ teaspoon cream of tartar

¾ cup heavy cream

2 tablespoons confectioners' sugar

Lemon rind, cut into thin strips, for garnish

Edible flowers and mint leaves, for garnish (optional)

It is the fresh lemon juice that makes this dessert as heavenly as it is!

In a 4-cup glass measure, combine the lemon juice, grated rind, egg yolks, and granulated sugar; beat with a spoon until well blended. Cook on HIGH for 3 to 4 minutes, stirring every minute until frothy. Pour into a large mixing bowl to cool and thicken. (Mixture may be put in the freezer at this point for 20 minutes to chill quickly.)

Place egg whites in a deep bowl. Beat with electric mixer until frothy; add cream of tartar and beat until stiff peaks form. Fold whites into cooled lemon mixture.

Pour cream into a deep bowl. Beat with electric mixer until thickened. Add confectioners' sugar and beat until just blended. Fold into lemon mixture.

Spoon mousse into 4 dessert glasses and place in freezer for 2 hours until solid. (If keeping longer, make sure to cover tightly in freezer. It can be stored up to 2 months.)

Drape lemon rind over the top before serving and garnish with edible flowers and mint leaves.

EDIBLE FLOWERS

Flowers that can be eaten will lift salads, main dishes, and desserts to new heights as well as make them more attractive. ❦ You may purchase edible flowers from specialty stores, but we find it more rewarding to grow our own. This is easily done in small gardens or window boxes and planters. Starting with herbs will give you the advantage of using both the leaves and flowers to enhance your menus. We like the blossoms from chives, oregano, basil, sage, borage, thyme, and mint. You may wish to add some of your own favorites. ❦ We plant borders of marigolds and nasturtiums to add a splash of color to the

garden and excitement to a wide variety of foods. We especially like the flavor of both the leaves and flowers that the nasturtium adds to salads and fish dishes. Marigolds make delightful fritters and add a lovely garnish to soups. ❦ We welcome spring by adding violet blossoms and dandelion petals to our dishes. They are followed with johnny jump-ups and pansies that produce flowers until the first frost. ❦ In early summer we take some of the flowers from our prolific zucchini patch and fill them with tasty stuffings. ❦ As soon as the honeysuckle vines start producing fragrant blossoms we add them to fruit desserts and salads, and we use their petals to make a sweet butter to spread onto tea sandwiches. ❦ It is important to know your edible flowers. For instance, the marigolds that we use in our recipes are pot marigolds (Calendula), not African marigolds (Tagetes), which are not to be eaten.

SAN DIEGO IN THE FALL

Serves 6

Salad of Warm Walnut-
Coated Goat Cheese

Nouvelle Deep-Dish
Seafood-and-Vegetable Pie

Frozen Raspberry Mousse
Cake with Balsamic-
Raspberry Coulis

SAN DIEGO IN THE FALL

Serves 6

Salad of Warm Walnut-Coated Goat Cheese

Nouvelle Deep-Dish Seafood-and-Vegetable Pie

Frozen Raspberry Mousse Cake with Balsamic-Raspberry Coulis

WINE SUGGESTION
California Fumé Blanc or French white Burgundy

The title describes the place where we received our inspiration for these dishes. San Diego has an array of warm salads, seafood in all fashions, and a relaxed atmosphere. We combined them all in this menu. It is a simple meal and all but the salad could be done over a week's time in advance.

PREPARATION PLAN

EARLIER IN THE DAY OR UP TO 1 WEEK IN ADVANCE:
1. Make the raspberry mousse and freeze.
2. Make the dessert sauce and refrigerate.

EARLIER IN THE DAY OR UP TO 2 DAYS IN ADVANCE:
1. Make the seafood pie filling and refrigerate if not using that day.
2. Make the Pâte Brisée (this could be made and frozen up to 2 weeks in advance).

EARLIER IN THE DAY OR UP TO 1 HOUR BEFORE SERVING:
1. Wash and dry the greens for the salad.
2. Coat the cheese with the walnuts.
3. Whisk together the dressing.

20 MINUTES BEFORE SERVING:
1. Reheat the seafood pie filling, if necessary.
2. Toss the salad greens with the dressing and arrange on the plates.

AT THE TABLE:
1. Heat the cheese and serve on the salad.
2. Serve the seafood pie.
3. Unmold the mousse cake and serve with the chilled sauce, or reheat the sauce on HIGH for 1 to 2 minutes if you want to serve it warm.

EVEN EASIER HINTS
Eliminate the raspberry mousse and just serve 1 quart raspberry sherbet with the Balsamic-Raspberry Coulis, and ½ pint heavy cream that has been whipped with 2 tablespoons confectioners' sugar, ½ teaspoon vanilla, and ⅛ teaspoon freshly ground black pepper.

MINT *Mint covers a wide variety of plants, all with a distinctive, crisp, clear flavor, varying in intensity. Best known are* Mentha peperita *or peppermint and* Mentha spicata *or spearmint. These pretty leaves are garnishes for meats and desserts. We love the fresh flavor mint gives to fish, poultry, and meats, as well as fresh and poached fruits and some vegetables, such as peas and artichokes. ❧ Mint will grow just about anywhere and if you don't cut it back, it will take over the entire garden.*

SALAD OF WARM WALNUT-COATED GOAT CHEESE

Serves: 6

Cooking time: 2 to 3 minutes

2 tablespoons walnut or olive oil
½ cup finely chopped walnuts
6 ounces goat cheese (Montrachet, Bucheron, Caprino, or Crottin) or mozzarella, cut into 6 (1-ounce) pieces (½ inch thick)
1 bunch arugula, washed and dried, or 1 cup other greens
1 small head radicchio or red-leaf lettuce, washed and dried
1 bunch watercress, washed and dried
1 small red onion, thinly sliced

DRESSING:
2 tablespoons white wine vinegar or lemon juice
⅓ cup olive oil
1 teaspoon grainy Dijon mustard
¼ teaspoon salt
¼ teaspoon freshly ground black pepper

Pour the oil into a custard cup. Place the chopped walnuts in a cereal bowl. Dip each side of a single piece of cheese into the oil, then into the nuts to coat evenly on all sides. Place the coated cheese around the outer rim of a 10-inch round microwaveproof plate. Set aside.

Combine the salad greens and onion in a medium bowl. Combine the dressing ingredients in a small bowl and whisk to blend. Just before serving, toss the salad greens with the dressing. Divide among six salad plates.

Place the cheese plate in the microwave oven and cook, uncovered, on MEDIUM for 2 to 3 minutes or until warm to the touch and just beginning to ooze out from the coating. With a spatula, place a piece of heated cheese on top of each salad.

NOUVELLE DEEP-DISH SEAFOOD-AND-VEGETABLE PIE

Serves: 6

Cooking time: About 40 minutes

Prepare the Pâte Brisée, cut into fish shapes, and bake.

In a 2-quart microwaveproof casserole, combine the ingredients up to the scallops. Cover tightly with the lid or plastic wrap turned back slightly on one side, and cook on HIGH for 15 to 20 minutes or until the carrots are tender, stirring twice.

Add the fish, peas, and cayenne. Cover again and cook on HIGH for 8 to 10 minutes, stirring once, until the fish is just cooked. Drain the cooking juices (you will have about 1½ cups) into a 4-cup glass measure and add the clam juice or water to equal 2 cups. Set aside.

Place the butter in a 1-cup measure and cook on HIGH for 40 seconds to 1 minute to melt. Stir in the flour to make a smooth paste. Stir into the cooking liquid. Cook, uncovered, on HIGH for 8 to 10 minutes or until boiling and thickened, whisking twice to make a smooth sauce. Stir into the fish-and-vegetable mixture. Sprinkle with the parsley. Cover and set aside until serving time.

To serve, spoon into six individual 2-cup ramekins or soup plates. Place 2 pastry fish on top of each and garnish with a sprig of thyme, if available.

NOTE: If you have made the filling in advance, reheat on HIGH for about 10 minutes or until heated through, stirring once. Be careful not to overheat and overcook the fish.

Pâte Brisée (recipe follows)
2 leeks, cleaned and (white part only) quartered and cut into ½-inch pieces
1 garlic clove, minced
½ pound small carrots, cut into ½-inch lengths
1 cup celery, cut into ¼-inch pieces
4 ounces fresh porcini or shiitake mushrooms, cut into ¼-inch slices
1 cup dry white wine
2 tablespoons tomato paste
1 tablespoon lemon juice
½ teaspoon dried thyme
¼ teaspoon salt
¼ teaspoon freshly ground black pepper
1 pound scallops
½ pound firm fish (sword, mako, tuna), cut into ½-inch cubes
1 (10-ounce) package frozen peas
Dash cayenne pepper
About ½ cup clam juice or water
2 tablespoons unsalted butter
2 tablespoons all-purpose flour
¼ cup chopped fresh parsley
6 sprigs thyme, for garnish (optional)

PÂTE BRISÉE

Makes: 12 large or 60 tiny shapes,
enough for 6 pot pies

Cooking time: 3 to 4 minutes

1 cup all-purpose flour
½ teaspoon salt
6 tablespoons very cold unsalted butter,
**   cut into 12 pieces**
3 to 4 tablespoons ice water

In a large mixing bowl or food processor, blend the flour and salt. Working quickly, cut the butter into the flour with a pastry blender, two knives, or a food processor until the particles are pea size. Add the water 1 tablespoon at a time, using a tossing motion to incorporate the dough, until the particles can be gathered lightly into a ball.

Flatten the dough into a pancake approximately 4½ inches in diameter. Cover with plastic wrap and freeze 30 minutes if in a hurry, or refrigerate for at least 1 hour or up to 3 days.

Roll the chilled dough into a ¼-inch-thick 12-inch circle. Using a cookie cutter (3 inches by 2 inches) or a knife, cut out 12 fish shapes or whatever else you fancy. Place the shapes in a circle on a large piece of double wax paper. Prick with a fork every ½ inch. Place the paper and pastry in the microwave oven and cook on HIGH for 3½ to 4 minutes or until opaque and dry but not brown, rotating the paper a half-turn halfway through the cooking.

Remove from the microwave oven and cool on a cooling rack.

NOTE: Packed tightly, dough keeps frozen for up to 2 weeks.

BALSAMIC-RASPBERRY COULIS

Makes: 1⅓ cups

Cooking time: 8 to 10 minutes

1 (12-ounce) package frozen raspberries
¼ cup sugar
⅛ teaspoon freshly ground black pepper
1 teaspoon balsamic vinegar

Combine all the ingredients in a 4-cup glass measure. Heat on HIGH for 8 to 10 minutes or until boiling, stirring once. Pass the mixture through a sieve to strain and remove the seeds. Pour into a jar and chill until serving time, or up to 1 week.

FROZEN RASPBERRY MOUSSE CAKE WITH BALSAMIC-RASPBERRY COULIS

Serves: 6

Cooking time: About 12 minutes

CRUST:
2 tablespoons unsalted butter
1 tablespoon sugar
½ cup finely ground almonds
1 egg, separated

MOUSSE:
1 (12-ounce) package frozen unsweetened raspberries
½ cup sugar
1 egg white
1 teaspoon lemon juice
¾ cup heavy cream, whipped
½ teaspoon vanilla extract

Balsamic-Raspberry Coulis (recipe precedes)
Mint leaves, for garnish (optional)

Place the butter in a medium microwaveproof bowl. Cook on HIGH for 40 seconds to 1 minute to melt. Stir in the sugar and nuts, then the egg yolk until well blended.

Cut a double thickness of wax paper to fit in the bottom of a microwaveproof loaf pan (9 inches by 5 inches). Press the almond mixture evenly into the pan. Heat on HIGH for 1 minute to set. Set aside.

Place the raspberries in a large microwaveproof bowl. Heat on DEFROST for 1 minute; break apart with a spoon. Add the sugar, egg white, and lemon juice, and beat together until well blended. Fold in the whipped cream and vanilla. Spoon onto the prepared crust. Cover the top with plastic wrap and freeze until hard, at least 4 hours or up to 2 weeks.

To serve, cut around the edges of the mousse loaf with a sharp knife, and invert onto a plate. Cut into slices and spoon a ribbon of Balsamic-Raspberry Coulis down the center of each slice. Garnish with a mint leaf, if available.

NEW ENGLAND ON THE HALF SHELL

Serves 6

Oysters on the Half Shell
with Sake Mignonette Sauce

Green Salad with Apples,
Walnuts, and Warm Maple
Vinaigrette

New Colony Chicken Pot
Pie with Red Wine and
Sweet Potatoes

Indian Pudding Timbales
with Warm Blueberry Sauce

NEW ENGLAND ON THE HALF SHELL

This menu was inspired by a visit to Boston and New England —the weather was crisp and the food warm and soothing. Many of the dishes are renditions of originals that are as old as our country, but all have a modern twist.

❡ Oysters are suggested but you may want to substitute chilled shrimp, a variation of the same recipe.

PREPARATION PLAN

THE DAY BEFORE:
1. Make the pot pie filling and refrigerate.
2. Make the Pâte Brisée (see page 168), and refrigerate. (This could be made and frozen up to 2 weeks in advance.)
3. Make the Indian pudding and refrigerate.

EARLIER IN THE DAY:
1. Wash and dry the salad greens.
2. Assemble and mix the salad dressing in a measuring cup.
3. Make the Mignonette Sauce.
4. Roll, cut into shapes, and bake the pâte brisée.

½ HOUR BEFORE SERVING:
1. Open the oysters.
2. Place the salad ingredients in a bowl. (Slice the apples while heating the salad dressing to make sure that they don't turn brown.)

3. Assemble the ingredients for the blueberry sauce; set aside.

AT THE TABLE:
1. Serve the oysters.
2. Heat and toss the salad and serve after the oysters are cleared. While eating the salad, heat the pie filling.
3. Assemble and serve the pot pies.
4. Heat the berry sauce while clearing the table, and unmold the puddings onto plates.

EVEN EASIER HINTS
1. Eliminate the oyster course.
2. Eliminate the Indian pudding and serve the Warm Blueberry Sauce over store-bought lemon sherbet.

WALNUT OIL *Walnut oil is delicious, and as you might imagine, very nutty in aroma and taste. It is sometimes preferred to olive oil when a heavier, sweeter oil is needed. If walnut oil is not used quickly, it turns rancid and thickens into more of a jelly than an oil.*

OYSTERS ON THE HALF SHELL WITH SAKE MIGNONETTE SAUCE

Serves: 6, with ⅔ cup sauce

Cooking time: Less than 1 minute

MIGNONETTE SAUCE:
2 tablespoons finely minced shallot
1 tablespoon finely minced carrot
1 teaspoon finely grated fresh ginger
1 tablespoon coarsely ground black pepper
¼ cup sake
¼ cup white wine vinegar

18 oysters

Now there is something to replace a strong arm and steady grip in the wrestling match with raw oysters in their shells —the microwave oven!

Combine all the sauce ingredients in a small bowl. Serve at once or chill for up to 4 hours.

To open the oysters, arrange 6 at a time, with the hinged sections toward the outside, around the outer rim of a 10-inch round microwaveproof plate. Leave space between each oyster. Cook on HIGH for 20 to 30 seconds or until the shells open just enough to insert a knife for opening. Repeat with the remaining oysters.

To serve, place 1½ tablespoons of the sauce in a small ramekin on each of six plates, along with 3 oysters.

Variation:

CHILLED SHRIMP WITH SAKE MIGNONETTE SAUCE: Eliminate the oysters. Combine 1 pound shrimp, preferably unpeeled, 1 minced garlic clove or 1 tablespoon finely chopped onion, 2 tablespoons lemon juice, 1 crushed bay leaf, and ½ teaspoon celery seed in a 9- or 10-inch round microwaveproof dish. Stir to coat the shrimp; then push the shrimp to the outer rim of the dish. Cover tightly with plastic wrap turned back slightly on one side, and cook on HIGH for 2½ to 6½ minutes or until the shrimp turn pink, stirring after 2 minutes to move lesser-cooked shrimp to the outside. Let stand, covered, for 2 to 3 minutes. Chill and serve to be peeled at the table, with Mignonette Sauce in small ramekins for dipping.

GREEN SALAD WITH APPLES, WALNUTS, AND WARM MAPLE VINAIGRETTE

Serves: 6

Cooking time: 2 minutes

6 cups salad greens (romaine or spinach)
2 large crisp apples (Cortland, Macoun, or Granny Smith), cored and thinly sliced just before assembling salad
¾ cup coarsely chopped walnut pieces

DRESSING:
¾ cup walnut or peanut oil
3 tablespoons white wine vinegar
3 tablespoons maple syrup
1 tablespoon Dijon mustard
¼ teaspoon freshly ground black pepper
¼ teaspoon salt (optional)

Wash and dry the salad greens. Place in a large salad bowl. Add the apples and walnuts to the greens.

Place the dressing ingredients in a 2-cup glass measure. Heat on HIGH for 1½ to 2 minutes or until warm but not boiling. Whisk to mix well. Toss with the greens, apples, and walnuts.

To serve, divide among six salad plates, making sure to spoon any dressing in the bottom of the bowl over the greens.

NEW COLONY CHICKEN POT PIE WITH RED WINE AND SWEET POTATOES

Prepare and bake 60 tiny star shaped cutouts of the Pâte Brisée (see illustration on page 170).

In a 3- or 4-quart microwaveproof casserole, combine the butter, oil, and garlic. Cover tightly with the lid or plastic wrap turned back slightly on one side, and cook on HIGH for 1½ to 2 minutes or until the butter is melted. Stir in the flour to make a smooth paste. Add the wine and stir. Cover again and cook on HIGH for 2 to 3 minutes to boil and slightly thicken.

Stir in the sweet potatoes and onions. Cover again and cook on HIGH for 12 to 14 minutes or until the potatoes are tender, stirring after 6 minutes.

Stir in the remaining ingredients except the tarragon for garnish. Cover and cook on HIGH for 20 to 22 minutes or until the chicken is tender, stirring after 10 minutes. Let stand, covered, for 10 minutes.

To serve, divide the pie filling among six 2-cup ramekins, terrines, or soup plates. Place 10 pastry cutouts on top of each and garnish with a sprig of tarragon.

NOTE: If you have made the filling in advance, reheat before assembling with the pastry. Heat, covered, on HIGH for 15 to 20 minutes, stirring every 5 minutes.

Serves: 6

Cooking time: About 40 minutes

Pâte Brisée (see page 168)
2 tablespoons unsalted butter
2 tablespoons olive oil
2 garlic cloves, minced
2 tablespoons all-purpose flour
1 cup dry red wine
1¼ pounds sweet potatoes, peeled and cut into 1-inch cubes
20 pearl onions, peeled, or 1 (16-ounce) package frozen
2 tablespoons tomato paste
1½ pounds skinless, boneless chicken (thighs or breasts, or a mixture of both), cut into 1-inch cubes
8 ounces mushrooms, quartered
1½ cups chicken broth or stock
2 tablespoons lemon juice
½ teaspoon freshly ground black pepper
½ teaspoon dried thyme
Salt to taste (optional)
2 sprigs fresh tarragon (4 inches long) or 1 teaspoon dried
6 sprigs fresh tarragon, for garnish (optional)

INDIAN PUDDING TIMBALES WITH WARM BLUEBERRY SAUCE

Serves: 6

Cooking time: 28 to 37 minutes

2 tablespoons unsalted butter
½ cup molasses
2 cups milk
¼ cup sugar
¼ cup cornmeal
1 teaspoon ground cinnamon
¼ teaspoon grated nutmeg
¼ teaspoon ground ginger
3 eggs, beaten
½ teaspoon vanilla extract
Warm Blueberry Sauce (recipe follows)

These individual cornmeal custards are spiced with cinnamon and bear the burnished hue of molasses. They are especially delicious with a spoonful of the Warm Blueberry Sauce.

Place the butter in a medium microwaveproof bowl. Heat on HIGH for 35 seconds to 1 minute or until melted. Set aside.

In a 3-quart microwaveproof casserole, combine the molasses, milk, sugar, cornmeal, cinnamon, nutmeg, and ginger. Cover tightly with the lid or plastic wrap turned back slightly on one side, and cook on HIGH for 5 to 10 minutes or until thickened, stirring once.

Meanwhile, beat the eggs into the melted butter. Slowly add the cooked molasses mixture to the eggs, stirring constantly. Stir in the vanilla. Pour into six 5- to 6-ounce microwaveproof custard cups or ramekins. Place the cups in the microwave oven in a circle with a 1-inch space between them. Cook, uncovered, on MEDIUM for 10 to 12 minutes or until a knife inserted ½ inch from the center comes out clean; reposition the custards once halfway through the cooking. Let stand for 10 minutes. Serve warm or chilled.

To serve, loosen the custards from the cups with a small sharp knife. Invert onto dessert plates and spoon the sauce over and around each pudding.

NOTE: It will be easier to get the cups in and out of the oven if you place them around the rim of a 12-inch round, flat microwaveproof plate.

WARM BLUEBERRY SAUCE

Combine all the ingredients in a 4-cup glass measure. If using fresh berries, cook on HIGH for 4 to 5 minutes or until just heated through, stirring once. Frozen berries will need 7 to 9 minutes. The berries are to be kept whole.

Makes: 2 cups

Cooking time: 11 to 14 minutes

2 cups fresh or 1 (12-ounce) package
    frozen unsweetened blueberries or
    huckleberries
2 tablespoons orange-flavored liqueur
1 tablespoon lemon juice

VALENTINE'S DAY

Serves 2

Chevre Salad with Walnut
Oil Dressing

French Baguette

Salmon Steaks with
Cucumber Roses and Caviar

Couscous and Chive
Timbales for Two

Berries, Chocolate Hearts,
and Cream

*W*hether you've been married twoscore years or are barely dating, a Valentine's Day can be made special with a little thought. A candlelit table, a single rose tied with lace, and a menu replete with seductive ingredients (we checked our dictionary of aphrodisiacs to make sure) all work together for a memorable evening.

The recipes are designed to keep you from slaving in the kitchen on this very special night. The delicate chocolate hearts and liqueur-infused cream dessert can be fashioned in advance, and the couscous cooked and molded up to a half-hour before serving. Even the goat cheese coated with walnuts (look for heart-shaped cheese) will be at the ready hours before its final quick heating. The rest . . . is up to you.

EARLIER IN THE DAY OR UP TO 1 HOUR BEFORE SERVING:

1. Prepare the chocolate hearts and pastry cream and refrigerate.
2. Wash and dry the lettuce.
3. Coat the cheese with the walnuts.

AT THE TABLE:

1. Toss the lettuce with the dressing. Heat the cheese and serve.
2. Cook the couscous and mold (see page 158).
3. Cook the salmon and serve with couscous.
4. Spoon cream and berries onto serving plates and garnish.

ARUGULA *Arugula, also called rocket, is a Mediterranean green which once grew wild and was free for the picking but now fetches a pretty price in American markets. Arugula has a piquant flavor, similar to young mustard greens. For the best flavor, use young fresh leaves, and use them soon after purchase, for they don't store well.*

CHEVRE SALAD WITH WALNUT OIL DRESSING

Serves: 2

Cooking time: 1 minute

3 tablespoons walnut or olive oil

2 tablespoons finely chopped walnuts

2 ounces goat cheese (Montrachet, Bucheron, Caprino, or Crottin), cut into 2 (1-ounce) pieces about ½ inch thick

1 small head radicchio or red-leaf lettuce

1 bunch arugula

1 very small red onion, thinly sliced

1 tablespoon white wine vinegar or lemon juice

Dash salt

Dash freshly ground black pepper

¼ French baguette, thinly sliced

Pour 1 tablespoon of the oil into a custard cup or small dish. Place the chopped nuts into another custard cup. Dip each piece of cheese into the oil, then into the nuts to coat evenly on all sides. Place the cheese on a small microwaveproof plate and set aside.

Wash and dry the radicchio and arugula. Combine in a bowl with the onion.

In a small bowl, combine the remaining 2 tablespoons oil, the vinegar, salt, and pepper. Just before serving, toss the dressing with the greens. Arrange on salad plates.

Cook the cheese on MEDIUM for 30 seconds or until warm to the touch and just a tiny bit of cheese starts to ooze out. Use a spatula to place each in the center of the salads on the plates and serve with thin slices of baguette.

SALMON STEAKS WITH CUCUMBER ROSES AND CAVIAR

Serves: 2

Cooking time: About 10 minutes

Place the salmon steaks in a 9- or 10-inch glass pie plate. Sprinkle with the Vermouth and pepper. Cover with wax paper and cook on MEDIUM for 4 minutes; turn over and continue to cook for 3 to 5 minutes more or until cooked through.

Meanwhile, with a swivel peeler, make 6 lengthwise peels of cucumber. Roll each up to form a "rose."

Remove the steak from the dish and place on serving plates, covering with foil to keep warm. Add the tomato and scallions to the cooking juices in the pie plate. Cover with wax paper and cook on HIGH for 2 to 3 minutes to heat through. Remove from the microwave oven, and stir in the butter until melted. Stir in the caviar. Spoon the sauce over the salmon. Top with the cucumber roses and serve.

2 salmon steaks (total ¾ pound)
2 tablespoons dry Vermouth
Freshly ground black pepper
1 English cucumber, washed, not peeled
½ cup peeled, seeded, and chopped tomato
2 tablespoons thinly sliced scallions
2 tablespoons unsalted butter, cut into ¼-inch cubes
1 tablespoon salmon caviar

BERRIES, CHOCOLATE HEARTS, AND CREAM

Serves: 2

Cooking time: 6 to 8 minutes

3 ounces semisweet chocolate pieces
¾ cup milk
¼ cup sugar
2 large egg yolks
2 tablespoons all-purpose flour
2 tablespoons orange-flavored liqueur
1 cup raspberries or strawberries

Line a cookie sheet with wax paper. Set aside.

Place the chocolate pieces in a Ziplock sandwich bag, moving all the pieces to one corner, but in a single layer. Cook on MEDIUM for 3 minutes to melt. (Push with fingers to feel that the chocolate is all very soft.) With a scissor, snip the corner off the part of the bag where the chocolate is melted and squeeze into 6 to 8 solid heart shapes onto the cookie sheet; these can be done free-form or into tiny cookie cutters. Let harden for at least ½ hour.

Meanwhile, pour the milk into a 2-cup glass measure. Cook on HIGH for 1½ to 2 minutes or until hot but not boiling.

In a 1-quart microwaveproof casserole, beat the sugar into the egg yolks with a whisk until well blended. Stir in the flour. Gradually add the heated milk, beating constantly. Cook on HIGH for 1 minute; beat with a whisk. Cook on HIGH for 1 to 2 minutes more or until thickened. Beat with a whisk and stir in the liqueur. Bring to room temperature. Chill until serving time.

To serve, divide the cream between two dessert plates. Sprinkle with ½ cup berries each; garnish with chocolate hearts.

SUPER BOWL

Serves 8

Irresistible Spiced Popcorn

Pâté en Croûte
and
Eggplant Caviar

Jambalaya

Crusty French Bread

Mixed Greens Salad with
Pecan Vinaigrette

Coffee Ice Cream with
Chocolate Shards and
Flaming Bourbon

Cookies

Basket of Fresh Fruit

SUPER BOWL

Serves 8

· First Quarter ·

Irresistible Spiced Popcorn

· Second Quarter ·

Pâté en Croûte
and
Eggplant Caviar

· Third Quarter ·

Jambalaya

Crusty French Bread

Mixed Greens Salad with
Pecan Vinaigrette

· Fourth Quarter ·

Coffee Ice Cream with
Chocolate Shards and
Flaming Bourbon

Cookies

Basket of Fresh Fruit

BEVERAGE SUGGESTION
Cold beer, California
Sauvignon Blanc, or chilled
Beaujolais-Villages

T his is a menu that we serve for casual entertaining like the Super Bowl, Emmy award night, après ski or hiking, or just for good friends. We have tailored the meal specifically to the four quarters of a football game; the Jambalaya can be made during the game or the day before and reheated. With a strong Cajun theme, if the Super Bowl is in New Orleans, you will really be "au courant." ¶ If football is not a cause for celebration in your house, you may want to serve this menu as a buffet, or serve the appetizers with drinks and follow with the main course, salad, and dessert served at the table.

PREPARATION PLAN

THE DAY BEFORE:
1. Make the Jambalaya and refrigerate.
2. Make the chocolate shards and freeze.
3. Make the Pâté en Croûte and refrigerate.
4. Make the Eggplant Caviar and refrigerate.
5. Wash and dry the salad greens, make dressing, and refrigerate.

THE DAY OF THE PARTY:
1. FIRST QUARTER— Make the popcorn (see page 142).
2. SECOND QUARTER —Slice and serve the pâté and Eggplant Caviar.
3. THIRD QUARTER— Reheat the Jambalaya. Toss the salad. Slice the bread.
4. FOURTH QUARTER —Scoop out the ice cream and serve with the chocolate shards, hot Bourbon, cookies, and fruit.

EVEN EASIER HINTS
1. Serve only fresh vegetable crudités (see page 122) and crackers instead of the pâté and Eggplant Caviar.
2. Eliminate the chocolate shards and purchase some really good chocolate and chop it coarsely.

CAYENNE *Cayenne (also called red pepper) is a red powder that is ground from the seeds and pods of various peppers grown in the Cayenne district of Africa. It has no relation to black or white pepper, and each container should be labeled "use with caution" for it has a real bite. It is a natural accent for everything from Bloody Marys to seafood and soufflés.*

PÂTÉ EN CROÛTE

Serves: 8

Cooking time: 12 minutes

2 slices bacon, diced

1 green onion, thinly sliced

1 garlic clove, minced

1 pound chicken livers

2 tablespoons unsalted butter, cut into
quarters

2 tablespoons brandy

¼ cup chopped fresh parsley

1 teaspoon grated fresh ginger or ½
teaspoon ground dried

½ teaspoon dry mustard

½ teaspoon dried thyme

½ teaspoon salt

¼ teaspoon marjoram

¼ cup shelled pistachios

Long loaf of French bread (about 16
inches long)

En croûte *means that something is encased in a crust. In this case, a liver pâté fragrant with brandy and herbs is packed into a hollowed-out loaf of French bread, which is then chilled and sliced for an attractive hors d'oeuvre.*

In a 2-quart microwaveproof casserole, combine the bacon, green onion, and garlic. Cook on HIGH for 2 minutes.

Add the chicken livers and cover tightly with the lid or plastic wrap turned back slightly on one side. Cook on MEDIUM for 10 minutes or until the livers are no longer pink, stirring once halfway through the cooking. Let stand, covered, for 5 minutes.

Spoon the liver mixture into the bowl of a food processor. Process until finely ground, then spoon into a medium mixing bowl. Add the remaining ingredients except the bread, and stir well to mix. Cover and chill thoroughly for about 6 hours.

Cut the ends from the bread, then cut the loaf in half crosswise. With the handle of a wooden spoon, push the soft center of the bread out of the loaf to within ½ inch of the crust. (Dry and make into bread crumbs for a later use.) Spoon the chilled pâté into the hollowed-out bread, packing well. Wrap each half in foil and chill.

To serve, unwrap the bread and slice into ½-inch pieces.

EGGPLANT CAVIAR

Makes: 2 cups

Cooking time: 5 to 7 minutes

Often called "poor man's caviar," the flavors and textures of this puree are luscious. Serve with crackers or on thinly sliced Daikon radish, cucumber, or zucchini.

Prick the whole eggplant in a few places with a fork and place it on a plate or paper towel. Cook on HIGH for 5 to 7 minutes or until softened. Let it cool in the refrigerator for about 30 minutes.

Cut the eggplant in half lengthwise, and scoop out the inside; discard the peel. Place the eggplant in the bowl of a food processor or blender or electric mixer. Process until the eggplant is pureed. Add the remaining ingredients and mix well. Pack into a serving bowl and chill until serving time.

To serve, place the crock on a large plate and surround with crackers or thin slices of lightly toasted French baguette and raw vegetables.

1 medium-size eggplant

1 medium-size ripe tomato, peeled, seeded, and finely chopped

1 medium-size onion, finely chopped

1 garlic clove, minced

1 tablespoon extra-virgin olive oil

1 tablespoon balsamic vinegar

1 teaspoon brown sugar

1 teaspoon chopped fresh ginger

½ teaspoon salt

¼ teaspoon freshly ground black pepper

JAMBALAYA

Serves: 6 to 8

Cooking time: 43 to 53 minutes

1 tablespoon olive or vegetable oil
2 garlic cloves, minced
2 medium onions, coarsely chopped
1 cup thinly sliced celery
1 bay leaf
1 teaspoon dried oregano
1 teaspoon dried thyme
1 teaspoon freshly ground black pepper
½ teaspoon salt or to taste
½ teaspoon cayenne pepper or to taste (up to 2 teaspoons)
2 cups long-grain rice
1 pound boneless, skinless chicken, cut into 1-inch cubes
2 cups canned clam juice or chicken broth
1 (16-ounce) can tomatoes, chopped and undrained
½ pound peeled shrimp
½ pound scallops
½ pound lean ham, cut into ½-inch cubes
½ pound smoked sausage such as kielbasa, cut into ½-inch slices and then halved or quartered depending on diameter
½ cup chopped fresh parsley

It is a common belief that the name for this delicious concoction comes from the French word for ham, jambon, *and an African word for rice,* ya. *In that case, the ham and rice are a must, but every recipe differs as to what other meats or fish are added, depending on availability, pocketbook, and desire. If you prefer a really "hot" dish, you may want to up the cayenne pepper.*

In a 4-quart microwaveproof casserole, combine the oil and garlic. Add the onions and celery. Cover tightly with the lid or plastic wrap turned back slightly on one side, and cook on HIGH for 3 minutes.

Stir in the bay leaf, oregano, thyme, black pepper, salt, and cayenne. Stir in the rice to coat well with the seasonings, then stir in the chicken. Add the broth and tomatoes. Cover tightly again and cook on HIGH for 10 to 15 minutes or until the liquid is boiling.

Stir in the remaining ingredients except the parsley. Cover again and cook on HIGH for 15 minutes or until the liquid is once again boiling; stir well. Re-cover and cook on MEDIUM for 15 to 20 minutes or until most of the liquid is absorbed and the rice is al dente, stirring once. Let stand for 5 minutes before serving.

NOTE: This reheats well. To reheat after refrigeration, cook on HIGH for 20 to 25 minutes, until heated through, stirring every 5 minutes, moving the cooler inner sections to the outside. (Add ½ cup more water or broth if mixture appears too dry; also try to keep the shrimp and scallops toward the center of the dish as much as possible to prevent overcooking.)

MIXED GREENS SALAD WITH PECAN VINAIGRETTE

Serves: 8

To prepare the greens in advance, wash and tear the greens and spread in a single layer on clean kitchen towels. Roll up and refrigerate for up to 24 hours.

Combine all the ingredients except the lettuce in a jar and shake well. Chill until serving time and shake again.

Place the greens in a bowl and toss with the dressing right before serving.

½ cup olive oil

⅓ cup wine vinegar

2 teaspoons grainy Dijon mustard

¼ teaspoon salt

¼ teaspoon freshly ground black pepper

½ cup coarsely chopped pecans

8 cups greens (such as red-leaf lettuce, curly endive [frisée], watercress, romaine, radicchio), washed, dried, and torn into bite-size pieces

BAY LEAF *Bay laurel or* Laurus nobilis *is native to the countries flanking the Mediterranean Sea. It is the same leaf as was used in wreaths for the winners of the Olympic Games, so is it any wonder that it symbolizes "glory."* ❦ *The whole leaf is a staple of a "bouquet garni," the packet of herbs often called for when one seasons soups and stews, and it is often referred to as the backbone of French cooking. You'll also find bay leaf in pickled foods and cured meats such as corned beef and pastrami. At the same time it adds a delicious flavor to custards and sweet sauces.* ❦ *Bay leaf has a sweet, peppery taste with a hint of clove and vanilla. It gives a provocative aroma to meat, fish, and fowl but can be overpowering when used in large quantities. Fresh bay leaves are beginning to appear in some specialty food markets. One medium-size leaf is adequate in recipes for six.*

COFFEE ICE CREAM WITH CHOCOLATE SHARDS AND FLAMING BOURBON

Serves: 8

Cooking time: About 3 minutes

6 ounces semisweet chocolate pieces
½ gallon good-quality coffee ice cream
½ cup Bourbon

Want to cause a sensation? Flame any dessert in front of your guests. There is something thrilling and terrifying about controlled fire. Don't try to flame all the Bourbon at once though, or you will have to invite the fire department to your party. (We did it and our container burned brightly for 15 minutes and permeated the house with a Bourbon scent for an evening.)

If you do choose to flambé, have a helper with a long match follow you around as you dispense the brandy and light each serving individually.

Leftover shards may be sealed and frozen to add a special touch to desserts at a later meal.

Place a sheet of wax paper on a cookie sheet and outline a 12- by 10-inch rectangle. Set aside.

Arrange the chocolate pieces in a circle in a microwaveproof cereal bowl, leaving the center free. Cook on MEDIUM for 2½ to 3½ minutes or until the chocolate is melted and shiny, stirring after 2½ minutes. Check after every 30 seconds after the first 2½ minutes to prevent scorching, because although the chocolate pieces still retain their shape, they may be soft enough to spread.

Spread the chocolate on the wax paper within the outline, smoothing with a spatula. Score well every 2 inches in one direction and every ½ inch in the other. Place in the freezer for 15 minutes to harden. Peel the wax paper from the chocolate and break along the scores. Place in a container and refreeze until serving time.

To serve, spoon the ice cream into bowls and decorate with the chocolate shards. Serve to the guests. Meanwhile, pour the Bourbon into a 4-cup glass measure and heat on HIGH for 35 seconds. Pour 1 tablespoon onto each serving of ice cream and ignite.

Variation:

COFFEE ICE CREAM AND FRENCH VANILLA ICE CREAM WITH CHOCO-LATE SHARDS AND CINNAMON: Use 1 quart coffee ice cream and 1 quart French vanilla ice cream; serve 1 scoop each side-by-side with chocolate shards and a dusting of ground cinnamon. Heated Bourbon may be added, if desired.

FRENCH BISTRO MENU

Serves 4

Chicory Salad with Hot
Bacon Vinaigrette

Fricassee of Cod with Red
Peppers and Parsleyed
Boiled Potatoes

French Bread

Crème Caramel with
Drunken Orange Segments

FRENCH BISTRO MENU

Serves 4

Chicory Salad with Hot
Bacon Vinaigrette

Fricassee of Cod with Red
Peppers and Parsleyed
Boiled Potatoes

French Bread

Crème Caramel with
Drunken Orange Segments

WINE SUGGESTION
California Chardonnay or
French white Burgundy

B istro food is nothing fancy but always satisfying. It brings a touch of France into your home for not much money, and that in itself is reason to celebrate. This menu requires little preparation, and it can all be done without advance preparation.

PREPARATION PLAN

1½ HOURS BEFORE SERVING:
1. Make the Crème Caramel with Drunken Orange Segments.
2. Cook the potatoes for the fricassee, and cut up the peppers and onions.
3. Cook the peppers and then add the fish.
4. While the fish is cooking, prepare the salad.

AT THE TABLE:
1. Heat the salad dressing and toss with greens and serve with bread.
2. Serve the fish with the vegetables.
3. Unmold custards and spoon on sauce to serve.

EVEN EASIER HINTS
1. Serve fresh fruit with cream, ice cream, or yogurt for dessert.
2. For early guests, have a little liverwurst on hand and spread it thinly over thin slices of baguette and top with little cornichons, fanned out. Serve with drinks.

CHICORY SALAD WITH HOT BACON VINAIGRETTE

Serves: 4

Cooking time: 5 minutes

1 large head chicory (frisé), washed, dried, and torn apart (makes about 4 cups)
6 ounces chunk lean bacon, diced into ½-inch pieces
1 medium-size red onion, thinly sliced
2 tablespoons red wine vinegar
1 teaspoon Dijon mustard
1 teaspoon sugar

Place the chicory in a salad bowl.

Place the bacon in a 4-cup glass measure. Cook on HIGH for 2 to 3 minutes, until cooked but not overly crisp. Remove the bacon pieces from the dish with a slotted spoon and spoon onto the lettuce.

Add the onion to the bacon fat. Cook on HIGH for 1 minute or until tender-crisp. Add the vinegar, mustard, and sugar. Cook on HIGH for 1 minute to heat through. Whisk well and pour over the lettuce. Toss and serve with slices of baguette.

FRICASSEE OF COD WITH RED PEPPERS AND PARSLEYED BOILED POTATOES

Serves: 4

Cooking time: 20 to 27 minutes

4 medium-size red-skinned boiling
    potatoes
¼ cup water
1 tablespoon olive oil
1 tablespoon unsalted butter
1 garlic clove, minced
1 large onion, thinly sliced
2 large red peppers, trimmed, seeded, and
    thinly sliced (about 2 cups)
1 teaspoon balsamic vinegar or lemon
    juice
¼ teaspoon dried thyme leaves
¼ teaspooon dried basil leaves
⅛ teaspoon fennel seed, crushed
¼ teaspoon freshly ground black pepper
¼ teaspoon salt or to taste
Dash cayenne pepper
1½ pounds cod fillets, cut into 4 serving
    pieces
1 teaspoon paprika
¼ cup chopped fresh parsley

With a vegetable peeler remove a circle of peel around the middle of each potato. Place them in a 1-quart dish with the water; cover tightly. Cook on HIGH for 6 to 10 minutes or until tender. Let stand, covered, until serving time.

In a 10-inch glass pie plate, combine the oil, butter, garlic, and onion; cook on HIGH for 1 minute. Stir in the peppers, vinegar, thyme, basil, fennel, black pepper, salt, and cayenne. Cover with plastic wrap turned back slightly on one side, and cook on HIGH for 4 to 5 minutes or until the peppers are tender, stirring once.

Stir again and place the cod fillets on top of the peppers around the outer rim of the plate with the thicker sections toward the outside. Cover again and cook on MEDIUM for 9 to 11 minutes, turning the fish over after 5 minutes.

To serve, divide the pepper mixture among four large ramekins or soup plates. Top with a cod fillet that has been sprinkled with a little paprika. Add a potato to each plate and sprinkle with the parsley.

CRÈME CARAMEL WITH DRUNKEN ORANGE SEGMENTS

Serves: 4

Cooking time: 13 to 15 minutes

2 large navel oranges, peeled and segmented
2 tablespoons orange-flavored liqueur
⅔ cup sugar
1 tablespoon water
1¼ cups milk
2 teaspoons vanilla extract
4 eggs

Combine the orange segments and liqueur in a small bowl and set aside.

Melt ⅓ cup of the sugar with the water in a 4-cup glass measure. Cook on HIGH for 2 minutes; stir. Cook for 3 minutes more or until the mixture develops a deep caramel color. Pour at once into four 5- or 6-ounce custard cups. Set aside.

Combine the milk and vanilla in a 4-cup glass measure on HIGH for 2 minutes or until hot but not boiling. Meanwhile, in a medium bowl, beat together the eggs and the remaining ⅓ cup sugar. Add the heated milk, pouring slowly and stirring constantly.

Pour the mixture into the prepared cups. Place the cups in the microwave oven with at least a 1-inch space between them. Cook, uncovered, on MEDIUM for 6 to 8 minutes or until firm, repositioning or rotating the dishes once or twice. Serve warm or chilled.

To unmold and serve, run a small knife around each custard cup and invert onto a serving plate. Spoon the orange segments and juices around the custard.

NOTE: Placing the custard cups on a large round plate will make removing and rotating the cups easier.

Brunch
for
All Seasons

Serves 6

Kir Royale or Nantucket
Red

Fall and Winter Fruit Cup
with Peppered Pink
Grapefruit Sorbet

Chili-Jack Cheese Timbales
on Frizzled Ham with
Tomato and Avocado

Steamed Pumpkin Bread
with Orange-Honey Cream
Cheese Spread

Coffee

BRUNCH FOR ALL SEASONS

This brunch menu can be varied depending on the season and the availability of different fruits. In spring, you can substitute the Spring and Summer Fruit Cup with Mango Sorbet (see page 210) for the fall and winter fruit cup. Steamed Raspberry-Apple Bread (see page 214) would be the choice for spring with Lemon-Honey Cream Cheese Spread (see page 215). The beverage this time will be found in the first two recipes.

PREPARATION PLAN

4 HOURS EARLIER OR THE NIGHT BEFORE:

1. Freeze the fruit for the sorbet.
2. Prepare the fruit cup mixture and refrigerate.
3. Make the bread and refrigerate if serving the next day.
4. Make the cream cheese spread and refrigerate.
5. Make Red Pepper Puree, if desired.

45 MINUTES BEFORE GUESTS ARRIVE:

1. Remove the cream cheese spread from the refrigerator.
2. Slice the loaves and tie with ribbons.
3. Prepare the timbale mixture and the custard cups.
4. Place the ham in the cooking dish.
5. Spoon the fruit into serving bowls or onto plates.

6. Peel and slice 1 avocado and slice 1 tomato; divide among six serving plates for the timbales.

WHEN GUESTS ARRIVE:

1. Mix and serve the Champagne drinks.
2. Put on the coffee.

15 MINUTES BEFORE SERVING:

Cook the timbales.

AT THE TABLE:

1. Process the sorbet and top the fruit; serve.
2. While clearing the fruit dishes, heat the ham.
3. Arrange the plates with the heated ham and top with the timbales.
4. If desired, reheat the bread before serving. Serve coffee.

CLOVES *The word* cloves *comes from the French "clou" meaning "nail," and indeed it does look like a small, reddish-brown nail. ❧ Cloves are the dried, unopened buds of an evergreen in the myrtle family. It is grown off the east coast of Africa and in the Philippines, but the Chinese had access to it as far back as 200 B.C. It was said that courtiers were required to chew on cloves while addressing the emperor, presumably to freshen the mouth. The oil of cloves might also have been used to give temporary relief to toothaches. ❧ Cloves are among the most pungent of spices, sweet and hot at the same time. Thus, in whole form, they can give gusto to soups or winter vegetables, and as a powder, flavor desserts and breads.*

KIR ROYALE

Serves: 6

1 ounce crème de cassis
24 ounces Champagne, well chilled

Measure ½ teaspoon crème de cassis into each of six Champagne flutes. Pour 4 ounces Champagne into each and serve immediately.

NANTUCKET RED

Serves: 6

12 ounces cranberry juice
1 ounce brandy
24 ounces Champagne

Measure 2 ounces cranberry juice and a dash brandy into each Champagne flute. Pour 4 ounces Champagne into each and serve immediately.

PEPPERED PINK GRAPEFRUIT SORBET

Makes: 6 large scoops

Cooking time: 2 minutes

Place the grapefruit segments in a single layer in a 2-quart microwaveproof dish. Place in the freezer to freeze solidly, at least 3 hours or overnight.

Place the dish in the microwave oven and heat on DEFROST for 2 minutes or until you can just break up the pieces. Place in the bowl of a food processor and process until finely chopped. Add the honey and process until smooth.

To serve, scoop into bowls and sprinkle with pepper, if desired.

NOTE: You may serve immediately or spoon into a container and freeze until serving time. If sorbet is too hard to scoop, remove cover from container and heat on DEFROST for 2 to 3 minutes. May be frozen for 2 weeks.

3 pink grapefruits, rinds removed, seeded, and segmented with membrane removed
3 tablespoons honey
Freshly ground black pepper (optional)

FALL AND WINTER FRUIT CUP WITH PEPPERED PINK GRAPEFRUIT SORBET

In a medium bowl, combine all the fruit and cover tightly. Refrigerate until serving time.

Place the fruit in six individual serving dishes and top each with a large scoop of sorbet.

Serves: 6

Cooking time: 2 minutes

1 cup seedless green grapes
1 cup seedless red grapes
1 cup orange segments
1 cup cubed pears
1 cup cubed apples
1 cup sliced bananas
Peppered Pink Grapefruit Sorbet (recipe precedes)

MANGO SORBET

Makes: 6 large scoops

Cooking time: 2 to 3 minutes

1 (1-pound) fresh mango, peeled, pitted,
 and cut into 1-inch pieces
2 tablespoons sugar
¼ cup yogurt
1 tablespoon orange-flavored liqueur
Freshly grated nutmeg

Place the mango in a single layer in a 2-quart rectangular microwaveproof dish. Freeze for 3 to 4 hours or overnight, until solid.

Place the dish in the microwave oven and heat on DEFROST for 2 to 3 minutes, until you can break up the pieces. Spoon the pieces into the bowl of a food processor. Pulse the processor on and off until the fruit is finely chopped. Add the remaining ingredients except the nutmeg, and continue to pulse at 15-second intervals until the mixture is blended and creamy.

Scoop into bowls and finish with a grating of fresh nutmeg.

SPRING AND SUMMER FRUIT CUP WITH MANGO SORBET

Makes: 6 servings

Cooking time: 2 to 3 minutes

1 cup strawberries
1 cup cubed pineapple
1 cup cubed honeydew melon
1 cup cubed cantaloupe
1 cup blueberries
1 cup cubed papaya, sliced kiwifruit, or
 raspberries
Mango Sorbet (recipe precedes)

If using fresh pineapple, reserve some of the leaves for garnish.

In a medium bowl, combine all the fruit and cover tightly. Refrigerate until serving time.

Spoon the fruit into six serving bowls and top each with a large scoop of sorbet.

CHILI-JACK CHEESE TIMBALES ON FRIZZLED HAM WITH TOMATO AND AVOCADO

Rub the bottom and sides of six custard cups well with the butter. Sprinkle the sides with the bread crumbs to coat well. Set aside.

Beat the eggs well in a medium bowl. Fold in the remaining ingredients except the Red Pepper Puree. Pour the mixture into the prepared custard cups. Place the cups around the outer rim of a 12-inch microwaveproof plate. Cover with wax paper. Cook on MEDIUM for 12 to 14 minutes or until a knife inserted close to the center comes out clean, rotating the plate twice if necessary. Let stand for 5 minutes.

To serve, run a knife between the timbales and the cups and turn out onto serving plates. Spoon a little Red Pepper Puree beside each, if desired. Place 2 slices each of avocado and tomato next to the puree.

Serves: 6

Cooking time: 12 to 14 minutes

1 tablespoon unsalted butter, cut into 6 pieces
¼ cup dry bread crumbs
3 eggs
1 (4-ounce) can mild green chilies, drained and chopped
6 ounces Monterey Jack cheese, grated
¾ cup half-and-half
¼ teaspoon freshly ground black pepper
Dash cayenne pepper
Red Pepper Puree (recipe follows) (optional)
1 large-size avocado, peeled, pitted and cut into 12 lengthwise slices
2 medium-size ripe tomatoes, cut into 12 crosswise slices

211

RED PEPPER PUREE

Makes: ¼ cup

½ cup Roasted Red Peppers (see page 294) or store-bought

Place the peppers in the bowl of a food processor or blender and process until smooth.

Spoon into the bottom corner of a plastic sandwich bag. Position the point over the soup, or food that you wish to garnish, and with a scissor cut the small tip off the baggie. Squeeze out a design.

FRIZZLED HAM

Serves: 6

Cooking time: 3 to 4 minutes

12 ounces lean ham, cut into 12 thin slices

This is a simple way to prepare ham, but because it crinkles up while it cooks, it forms an attractive bed for egg timbales or even scrambled eggs.

Separate the ham and arrange in overlapping slices around the outside of a 10-inch glass pie plate. Cover with wax paper and cook on HIGH for 3 to 4 minutes or until heated through, stirring after 2 minutes.

To serve with Chili-Jack Cheese Timbales, divide the ham among six plates and unmold a timbale on top of the ham.

STEAMED PUMPKIN BREAD

Try this at your next Thanksgiving dinner. It's delicious and adds a special touch.

Combine the dry ingredients in a large bowl; mix well. Add the wet ingredients, stirring to blend. Cut two circles of wax paper to fit the inside bottom of a 2-cup glass measuring cup. Spoon in half the batter, which will reach the 1½-cup mark.

Combine the topping in a small bowl. Sprinkle half on top of the batter. Cover with plastic wrap turned back slightly on one side, and cook on MEDIUM for 8 to 10 minutes or until a toothpick inserted in the center comes out clean, rotating a half-turn halfway through the cooking. Let stand, directly on the counter, for 5 to 10 minutes.

Repeat the same procedure to make a second loaf. With a knife, loosen the cooked loaves from the dishes and turn out. Serve immediately, or cool and wrap in plastic wrap and refrigerate for the next day.

To serve: When the bread has cooled well, stand it up so that it looks like a flowerpot. With a serrated or very sharp knife, cut it vertically into 8 wedges. Reassemble and tie together with a nonmetallic ribbon (to allow for reheating the bread). Bring to the table on a leaf-lined plate. If you have any edible flowers or mint, orange, or lemon leaves and long strips of lemon or orange rind), you may wish to top the pot with them. To serve, untie the ribbon and pass with cream cheese spread.

NOTE: The bread can be reheated after being sliced and tied with ribbon. Heat the 2 loaves on HIGH for 1 minute.

Makes: 2 small loaves to serve 6

Cooking time: 8 to 10 minutes

DRY INGREDIENTS:
½ cup yellow cornmeal
½ cup whole wheat flour
½ cup all-purpose flour
½ teaspoon salt
½ teaspoon baking powder
½ teaspoon baking soda
½ teaspoon cinnamon
¼ teaspoon cloves
¼ teaspoon nutmeg

WET INGREDIENTS:
2 tablespoons grated orange rind
½ cup golden raisins
½ cup coarsely chopped walnuts
1 cup pureed pumpkin
½ cup molasses
1 egg, beaten

TOPPING:
2 tablespoons coarsely chopped walnuts
½ teaspoon cinnamon
Orange-Honey Cream Cheese Spread
   (recipe follows)

STEAMED RASPBERRY-APPLE BREAD

Makes: 2 small loaves to serve 6

Cooking time: 8 to 10 minutes

DRY INGREDIENTS:

½ cup yellow cornmeal

½ cup whole wheat flour

½ cup all-purpose flour

½ teaspoon salt

½ teaspoon baking powder

½ teaspoon baking soda

WET INGREDIENTS:

1 teaspoon vanilla extract

1 tablespoon grated lemon rind

½ cup dark brown sugar

½ cup golden raisins

½ cup coarsely chopped pecans

1 cup applesauce

1 cup raspberries, rinsed and drained

TOPPING:

2 tablespoons coarsely chopped walnuts

½ teaspoon cinnamon

Lemon-Honey Cream Cheese Spread
    (recipe follows)

Combine the dry ingredients in a large bowl; mix well. Add the wet ingredients, stirring to blend. Cut two circles of wax paper to fit the inside bottom of a 2-cup glass measuring cup. Spoon in half the batter, which will reach the 1½-cup mark.

Combine the topping in a small bowl. Sprinkle half on top of the batter. Cover with plastic wrap turned back slightly on one side, and cook on MEDIUM for 8 to 10 minutes or until a toohpick inserted in the center comes out clean, rotating a half-turn halfway through the cooking. Let stand, directly on the counter, for 5 to 10 minutes.

Repeat the same procedure to make a second loaf. With a knife, loosen the cooked loaves from the cups and turn out. Serve immediately, or cool and wrap in plastic wrap and refrigerate for the next day.

To serve, follow the serving suggestions for Steamed Pumpkin Bread (recipe precedes).

NOTE: The 2 loaves can be reheated on HIGH for 1 minute.

ORANGE-HONEY CREAM CHEESE SPREAD

Unwrap the cream cheese and place it in a medium microwaveproof bowl. Heat on DEFROST for 1 to 2 minutes to soften. Beat in the remaining ingredients. Spoon into a serving dish or put into a pastry bag and pipe it onto one plate or individual plates. Refrigerate until serving time.

Variation:

LEMON-HONEY CREAM CHEESE SPREAD: Substitute 1 teaspoon grated lemon rind for the orange rind, and 1 teaspoon vanilla for the cinnamon.

Makes: About 1 cup

Cooking time: 1 to 2 minutes

1 (8-ounce) package cream cheese
3 tablespoons honey
1 teaspoon grated orange rind
½ teaspoon ground cinnamon

NEW AMERICAN DINNER (WITH SOUTHWESTERN TWIST)

Serves 4

Guacamole with Crunchy
Jicama and Carrot Batons

Nouvelle Crab Cakes

Papaya-Cilantro Salsa

Spoon Bread

Cinnamon Pastry Flowers
with Ice Cream and
Raspberries

Guacamole with Crunchy
Jicama and Carrot Batons

Nouvelle Crab Cakes

Papaya-Cilantro Salsa

Spoon Bread

Cinnamon Pastry Flowers
with Ice Cream and
Raspberries

WINE SUGGESTION
California Chardonnay or
Sauvignon Blanc, a Mexican
beer, or, depending on your
day, Heradura Margaritas

New American Dinner (with Southwestern Twist)

*T*his meal is just so delicious and satisfying that we make it for family and friends on Friday evenings after a busy work week. We haven't sent anyone away from the table yet who didn't feel restored in body and soul. ❡ If you do plan to do it all in one night, allow about 2 hours before serving, and either make the pastry before as directed or eliminate it and substitute cookies.

PREPARATION PLAN

2 DAYS BEFORE:
Make the pastry dough and refrigerate.

THE DAY BEFORE:
1. Cook the pastry flowers and after cooling, wrap up and keep at room temperature until needed.
2. Make the Raspberry Sauce and refrigerate.
3. Make the salsa and refrigerate.

1¼ HOURS BEFORE SERVING:
1. Prepare the crumbs for the crab cakes.
2. Mix the crab cakes.
3. Cut the red pepper for the spoon bread.
4. Cut the carrots and jicama, and wash the radicchio for the guacamole.

45 MINUTES BEFORE SERVING:
1. Cook the spoon bread; let stand, covered.

2. Meanwhile, form the crab cakes.
3. Mix up the guacamole.

AT THE TABLE:
1. Arrange the guacamole on plates or a platter and serve.
2. While clearing the guacamole course, cook the crab cakes.
3. Reheat the spoon bread, if necessary.
4. Arrange the crab cake plates with 2 scoops of spoon bread and the red pepper. Pass the salsa at the table.
5. Fill pastry cups, garnish, and serve.

EVEN EASIER HINTS
Eliminate the pastry shells, and purchase cinnamon cookies to be served with ice cream and berries, and if desired, Raspberry Sauce.

PAPRIKA *Paprika is the ground powder of a sweet red pepper plant native to Central America, which Spanish explorers brought back to their country. Today most paprika still comes from Spain and Central Europe. Not only does this spice add the unique flavor and color found in Chicken Paprikash and Hungarian Goulash, but it lends a nutritional edge with high amounts of vitamins A and C.*
❦ *Paprikas vary in color and flavoring, existing in various vibrancies of reddish orange with flavors ranging from mild and slightly sweet, to pungent. Look for Hungarian paprika for the highest quality.*

GUACAMOLE WITH CRUNCHY JICAMA AND CARROT BATONS

Serves: 4 (about 2 cups)

2 ripe avocados (Hass preferred)
1 small ripe tomato, finely chopped
1 tablespoon minced onion
4 tablespoons lime juice
Freshly ground black pepper to taste
1 head radicchio, separated and washed
1 jicama, peeled and julienned into thin
    strips
1 large carrot, peeled and julienned into
    thin strips
Blue corn chips or regular corn chips

This can be served either as a dip with cocktails or as a first-course salad. The jicama is a brown-skinned tuber with a crisp white flesh that is juicy and mild.

Right before serving, coarsely mash the avocados with a nonmetal spoon in a medium bowl. Fold in the tomato, onion, and lime juice. Pepper to taste.

If serving as a salad course, line each of four salad plates with the radicchio. Spoon ¼ of the guacamole into the center and surround with the jicama and carrot strips. Pass the corn chips. If serving as a dip, arrange the radicchio on one large platter with the guacamole in the center and the jicama, carrots, and chips around the outside.

NOUVELLE CRAB CAKES

Combine the bread crumbs with the paprika and parsley. Set aside.

Place the butter in a 9-inch glass pie plate, and cook on HIGH for 35 seconds to 1 minute to melt. With a fork, stir in the bread crumbs to blend. Even out the crumbs and cook on HIGH for 2 minutes to toast; stir. Cook on HIGH for 30 seconds to 1 minute more. Set aside.

In a large bowl, combine the remaining ingredients except the garnish. Refrigerate until ready to cook. (These two steps can be done up to 1 day in advance.)

Before cooking, even up to 1 hour before, pack ¼ of the mixture at a time into a 6-ounce custard cup to make a compact cake. Turn the cakes out around the outside of a 10- or 12-inch round microwaveproof plate, flattening them slightly into even cakes that are 3½ inches in diameter by ¾ inch thick.

Sprinkle each cake evenly with about 2 tablespoons of the bread crumbs. Cover with a paper towel and cook on HIGH for 8 to 10 minutes or until heated through.

To serve, place 1 cake onto each serving plate; top with a sprig of parsley and a slice of lemon.

Serves: 4

Cooking time: 11 to 14 minutes

2 slices good-quality white bread with crusts, toasted, cut into quarters, processed into about ¾ cup bread crumbs
½ teaspoon paprika
2 tablespoons finely chopped fresh parsley
2 tablespoons unsalted butter
1 pound cooked lump crabmeat, picked over with cartilage removed
¼ cup mayonnaise
2 tablespoons lemon juice
1 large egg yolk, beaten
¼ cup finely chopped green onion or chives
½ teaspoon dry mustard
⅛ teaspoon cayenne pepper
Fresh lemon slices and parsley, for garnish

PAPAYA-CILANTRO SALSA

Makes: 1 cup

1 large ripe papaya (about 1 pound),
    peeled and seeds removed
2 tablespoons chopped onion
¼ cup chopped fresh coriander (cilantro)
1 jalapeño pepper, seeds removed and
    chopped
2 tablespoons lime juice
¼ teaspoon salt

Cut the papaya into cubes and place in the bowl of a food processor. Process with the remaining ingredients into a coarse salsa, or chop the papaya cubes and mix all the ingredients by hand. Cover and refrigerate until ready to use.

NOTE: The salsa may be made 1 day in advance.

Variation:

PEAR-CILANTRO SALSA: Substitute 2 ripe (about 1 pound) peeled and cored pears for the papaya.

CORIANDER

Fresh coriander, or, by other names, Mexican cilantro or Chinese or Indian parsley, is one of the oldest and most widely grown herbs in existence. It looks like Italian flat parsley but you'll know the minute you take a whiff that you're holding pungent cilantro. ❦ *To get the most from this fresh herb, it is best to cut and serve at the last minute, since its flavor dissipates quickly after cutting. It is very fresh and clean in flavor, almost lemony, adding sparkle to cooked foods unlike almost any other herb we can think of.*

SPOON BREAD

This is a rich corn pudding that makes a beautiful marriage with crab cakes. Using an ice cream scoop, we place 2 scoops onto each serving plate along with a fan of crisp red pepper strips.

In a 2-quart glass measure or microwaveproof casserole, combine all the ingreddients except the eggs. Cover with wax paper and cook on HIGH for 3 minutes; stir well. Cover again and continue to cook on HIGH for 3 to 4 minutes more, stirring every minute until most of the liquid is absorbed by the cornmeal.

Add about ½ cup of this mixture to the eggs, stirring well to equalize the temperature. Slowly stir back into the remaining mixture. Cover with wax paper and cook on HIGH for 2 minutes; stir. Cover again and cook on HIGH for 2 minutes more; stir.

Smooth the top, cover again, and cook on MEDIUM for 2 to 4 minutes or until set. Let stand, covered, until ready to serve.

Spoon onto plates next to crab cakes and garnish with red pepper.

NOTE: This can be cooked in advance and reheated later on MEDIUM for 6 to 8 minutes.

Makes: 4 servings

Cooking time: 12 to 15 minutes

3 tablespoons unsalted butter
1½ cups milk
1 cup fresh or frozen corn (preferably white shoe peg or other sweet white variety)
½ cup cornmeal
1 teaspoon sugar
½ teaspoon salt
⅛ teaspoon cayenne pepper
3 large eggs, beaten
1 red pepper, seeded and thinly sliced lengthwise or chopped

CINNAMON PASTRY FLOWERS WITH ICE CREAM AND RASPBERRIES

Serves: 4

Cooking time: About 10 minutes

1 cup all-purpose flour

2 tablespoons sugar

½ teaspoon ground cinnamon

3 tablespoons solid vegetable shortening

3 tablespoons very cold unsalted butter,
    cut into 12 pieces

2 to 3 tablespoons ice water

2 cups fresh raspberries, strawberries, or
    blueberries

1 pint vanilla ice cream, lemon or lime
    sherbet, or frozen yogurt

Raspberry Sauce (see page 60)

In a large mixing bowl blend the flour, sugar, and cinnamon. Working quickly, cut the shortening into the flour with a pastry blender or two knives until the particles are pea size. Cut in the butter. Add the water, 1 tablespoon at a time, using a tossing motion to incorporate it into the dough until the particles can be gathered into a ball. If using a processor, mix flour, sugar, and cinnamon by pulsing twice. Add shortening and butter and pulse six to eight times until particles are pea size. Turn on processor and slowly pour water into tube. As soon as the mixture is the consistency of coarse cereal, turn off processor and, with a rubber spatuala, transfer mixture to a large square of plastic wrap. Form a ball by pulling plastic wrap together (this keeps dough from being overworked).

Flatten the dough into a 4½-inch square. Wrap with plastic wrap and chill for at least 1 hour or up to 3 days.

On a lightly floured surface, roll out the chilled dough into a 12-inch square. (A roller stocking on a rolling pin or a marble rolling pin will make this process easier, requiring less additional flour.) Cut four 4-inch squares of pastry and prick every ½ inch with a fork.

Invert four 6- or 7-ounce custard cups onto a 12-inch microwaveproof plate. Top each custard cup with a circle of wax paper slightly larger then the top of the cup. Center a pastry square over each cup, allowing the points to hang over the sides to form a 4-pointed "flower." Cook on HIGH for 5 to 7 minutes or until the pastry is opaque and dry, rotating the whole dish after 3 minutes. Let cool for 5 minutes.

Very gently loosen the edges of the crust with a sharp knife and lift the shells. Peel away the wax paper and place the pastry flowers onto serving plates.

Divide the berries among the pastry cups. Top with a small scoop of ice cream. Spoon some of the Raspberry Sauce onto the serving plate and drizzle onto the ice cream.

CASUAL CHOUCROÛTE GARNIE

Serves 6

Wild Mushroom Pâté
with
Large Garlic-Thyme
Croutons

Choucroûte Garnie

Pumpernickel Bread

Parsleyed Potatoes

Normandy Apple Tart

CASUAL CHOUCROÛTE GARNIE

This is a hearty, casual menu for late fall or winter, which we like to serve after a walk or cross-country skiing. The menu is easy to assemble and even travels well to a country home. ❦ With a meal this informal, we eliminate the first course and serve the mushroom pâté with drinks. You may choose to eliminate the dessert and serve instead pears, apples, nuts, and cheeses, including a nice ripe Brie.

PREPARATION PLAN

THE DAY OR NIGHT BEFORE:

1. Make the pastry dough, pastry cream, and Caramel Sauce, and refrigerate.
2. Make the mushroom pâté and refrigerate.
3. Bake the apple tart; cool and refrigerate.
4. Make two batches of Large Garlic-Thyme Croutons (see page 273).

1½ HOURS BEFORE SERVING:

1. Make the Choucroûte Garnie.
2. Make the potatoes during the standing time of the choucroûte.

AT THE TABLE:

1. Serve the pâté and croutons while the choucroûte is still cooking.
2. Slice the pumpernickel for the choucroûte.

3. Serve the choucroûte, potatoes, and bread.
4. Bring the tart and Caramel Sauce to room temperature and serve.

EVEN EASIER HINTS

1. Eliminate croutons and serve with crackers.
2. Eliminate the tart and serve Warm Apple Slices over Ice Cream (see page 235), or simply serve a selection of fruits and cheeses.

CARAWAY SEEDS

Caraway seeds are believed to have been in existence for over 5,000 years. As recorded in a medical papyrus in Thebes, the seeds are said to aid the digestion, which may be some of the attraction of "aquavit," the caraway-flavored Scandinavian liqueur, as a libation with the likes of pickled herring. ❦ You will detect its aromatic anise flavor in Hungarian beef or German stews, and often in boiled cabbage, potatoes, and coleslaw.

WILD MUSHROOM PÂTÉ

Makes: About 2 cups

Cooking time: 7 to 8 minutes

2 tablespoons unsalted butter
½ cup thinly sliced scallions
1 pound fresh mushrooms (chanterelles or
    porcini preferred, or ½ pound of
    these plus ½ pound domestic
    mushrooms), sliced
2 tablespoons Madeira or brandy
½ teaspoon salt
½ teaspoon freshly grated nutmeg
½ cup sour cream or plain yogurt
¼ teaspoon freshly ground black pepper
½ cup coarsely chopped hazelnuts
2 tablespoons chopped chives or parsley

This is a mouth-watering pâté with a woodsy scent that is delectable on Large Garlic-Thyme Croutons.

In a 2-quart microwaveproof casserole, combine the butter and scallions. Cook on HIGH for 2 minutes. Stir in the mushrooms. Cook, uncovered, on HIGH for 5 to 6 minutes or until the mushrooms cook down and are slightly darkened.

Spoon the mushrooms into the bowl of a food processor. Add the remaining ingredients except the nuts and chives, and process until smooth. Remove the blade from the bowl, or transfer mixture to a separate bowl, and fold in the nuts.

Pack the mixture into a crock, serving bowl, or small new clay flowerpots. Chill overnight or up to 1 week to develop the flavors. Sprinkle with the chives and serve on croutons and/or crackers.

CHOUCROÛTE GARNIE

This classic Alsatian dish is a combination of pickled white cabbage and smoked meats cooked with white wine, caraway, and onions. It is a hearty winter dish that can easily be made in advance.

I n a 4-quart microwaveproof casserole, combine the bacon, onions, and garlic. Cook on HIGH for 4 to 5 minutes or until the onions are tender and the bacon is partially cooked.

Stir in the remaining ingredients except the meats and potatoes. Cover tightly with the lid or plastic wrap turned back slightly on one side, and cook on HIGH for 10 to 12 minutes or until the liquid is boiling; stir.

Transfer half the sauerkraut to a plate for a moment and arrange the meats over the sauerkraut remaining in the casserole, with the thicker sections to the outside. Spoon the sauerkraut back over the meat. Cover again with the lid and cook on HIGH for 10 minutes, then on MEDIUM for 30 minutes or until the meat is heated through and the flavor of the dish developed.

Let stand, covered, for 10 to 15 minutes. In the meantime, cook the potatoes. Serve with boiled Parsleyed Potatoes and pumpernickel bread.

Serves: 6

Cooking time: About 1 hour

2 ounces slab bacon, rind removed and cut into ½-inch cubes
2 medium-size onions, thinly sliced
2 garlic cloves, minced
3 pounds sauerkraut, rinsed
1½ cups chicken broth
1 cup dry white wine
1 large apple, cored but not peeled and thinly sliced
½ teaspoon caraway seed
½ teaspoon dried thyme
½ teaspoon freshly ground black pepper
1 bay leaf
6 smoked pork chops
6 links smoked bratwurst or kielbasa
Parsleyed Potatoes (recipe follows)

231

PARSLEYED POTATOES

Serves: 6

Cooking time: 8 to 10 minutes

2 pounds small red potatoes, about 1½ to 2 inches in diameter, washed with a single strip peeled around the middle
¼ cup water
¼ cup chopped fresh parsley

Not only is this center peel around the potatoes decorative, but it also eliminates the need to pierce them.

In a 2-quart microwaveproof casserole, combine the potatoes and water. Cover tightly with the lid or plastic wrap turned back slightly on one side, and cook on HIGH for 8 to 10 minutes or until the potatoes are tender.

Let stand, covered, for 3 minutes. Drain and arrange on a platter with the Choucroûte Garnie, and sprinkle the potatoes with parsley.

THYME *A perennial of the mint family, thyme is a flowering plant that beautifies many rock gardens; it is also the gray-green leaves that adorn many a stew.* ❨ *Thyme is native to the United States and southern Europe and was brought to England by the Romans, yet France remains the leading producer. It is one of the most versatile herbs and it has a distinctively sweet aroma and slightly pungent flavor. It is one of the most versatile herbs. Commercially it is found in French Benedictine liqueur and thyme honey is prized by connoisseurs. Thyme is especially good in salads and with potatoes or tomatoes, with fish and in fish chowders, and with lamb.*

NORMANDY APPLE TART

Serves: 6

Cooking time: About 25 minutes

Basic Flaky Pastry Dough (recipe follows)
Vanilla Pastry Cream (recipe follows)
1½ pounds firm tart apples (Granny Smith), cored, peeled, and cut into ¼-inch-thick slices
1 tablespoon lemon juice
⅓ cup apricot preserves
Caramel Sauce (recipe follows)

The combination of flaky pastry cradling apple slices in pastry cream, napped in rich Caramel Sauce, is not to be missed. All can be made a day in advance and refrigerated. To bring the tart to room temperature, place it in the microwave oven on HIGH for 1 minute. The flavors are best when served at room temperature!

While the dough is chilling, make the pastry cream and chill.

In a bowl, toss the apples with the lemon juice.

Cut out a 14-inch double square of wax paper. On a lightly floured surface, roll out the chilled dough into a 12-inch circle (a marble rolling pin or a roller stocking on a rolling pin makes this process easier). Using a 10-inch plate as a guide, cut a 10-inch-diameter circle from the dough. With the excess dough, cut ½-inch-wide crescents with a small round or crescent-shaped cookie cutter. Arrange these crescents on the outside edge of the pastry, overlapping them to make a ½-inch-thick rim.

Prick the pastry with a fork every ½ inch. Place the pastry on the wax paper and cook on HIGH for 6 to 8 minutes or until opaque, rotating once. Let stand for 10 minutes. Remove the wax paper and place the pastry on a 12-inch microwaveproof plate. (If the pastry breaks in one or two areas, push it together and the pastry cream will glue it together—no one will ever know!)

Spread the pastry cream evenly inside the ½-inch rim. Arrange the apples in overlapping concentric circles on top of the pastry cream, beginning from the outer edge. Cover with wax paper and cook on HIGH for 6 to 8 minutes, until the apples are tender. Let cool for 10 to 15 minutes.

Place the apricot jam in a 1-cup glass measure and melt it on HIGH for 1 to 1½ minutes. Brush evenly over the apple slices.

BASIC FLAKY PASTRY DOUGH

Makes: Enough for 1 tart

1 cup all-purpose flour
3 tablespoons solid vegetable shortening
3 tablespoons very cold unsalted butter,
    cut into 12 pieces
1 tablespoon cider vinegar

Place the flour in a large mixing bowl or food processor bowl. Working quickly, cut the shortening into the flour with a pastry blender, two knives, or the food processor blade until the particles are pea size. Cut in the butter. Add the vinegar, using a tossing motion or the food processor to incorporate it into the dough. (If you are using a food processor, you will need to place the particles on a piece of plastic wrap at this point and push them together.)

Flatten the dough into a 4½-inch pancake. Wrap with plastic wrap and chill for at least 1 hour or up to 3 days.

VANILLA PASTRY CREAM

Makes: About 1 cup

Cooking time: About 5 minutes

1 cup milk
1 large egg
¼ cup sugar
2 tablespoons cornstarch
1 teaspoon vanilla extract

Pour the milk into a 1-cup glass measure. Cook on HIGH for 1 to 2 minutes to steam but not boil.

In a 1-quart bowl, combine the egg, sugar, and cornstarch. Gradually whisk the heated milk into the egg mixture, beating constantly. Cook on HIGH for 1 minute; beat. Cook on HIGH for 1 minute more or until the cream thickens and almost begins to boil, stirring at 30-second intervals. Stir in the vanilla. Place plastic wrap directly on the surface of the cream to keep a skin from forming. Chill until ready to use.

CARAMEL SAUCE

Makes: ¾ cup

Cooking time: 4 minutes

½ cup brown sugar
½ cup heavy cream
2 tablespoons light corn syrup

This is rich and sweet—2 tablespoons over cinnamon ice cream also is luscious. If you make it a day in advance and refrigerate, this sauce can be brought to room temperature by heating it on HIGH for 1 minute.

Combine all the ingredients in a 4-cup glass measure; whisk to blend. Cook on HIGH for 2 minutes; whisk. Cook on HIGH for 1 minute more; whisk. Cook on HIGH for 1 minute more or until slightly thickened and caramel colored; whisk well until the mixture stops boiling. (It will thicken as it cools.)

WARM APPLE SLICES OVER ICE CREAM

Serves: 6

Cooking time: About 7 minutes

4 tablespoons unsalted butter
¼ cup brown sugar
4 ounces brandy
1 tablespoon lemon juice
½ teaspoon ground cinnamon (only if not
    serving over cinnamon ice cream)
4 tart cooking apples, peeled, cored, and
    cut into ¼-inch slices
1 quart vanilla or cinnamon ice cream

Place the butter in a 9-inch glass pie plate. Heat on HIGH for 35 seconds to 1 minute to melt. Stir in the brown sugar, 2 ounces of the brandy, the lemon juice, and cinnamon. Stir in the apples and coat well with the mixture. Cover with wax paper and cook on HIGH for 6 to 7 minutes or until the apples are tender.

Pour the remaining 2 ounces brandy in a 1-cup glass measure. Heat on HIGH for 15 seconds. Pour over the apples and light with a match. Spoon while still flaming over ice cream.

TREE-TRIMMING PARTY

Serves 6 to 8

Italian Cheese Dome

Breast of Veal Stuffed with
Peppers and Basil

Pasta with Mushrooms

Bread Sticks

Frisée with Warm Balsamic
and Pine Nut Vinaigrette

Spiced Poached Pears with
Ice Cream

Christmas Cookies

Sambuca-Espresso Truffles

TREE-TRIMMING PARTY

This is a cozy and comforting meal that we save for special friends right before the holidays. The red and green in the cheese dome and stuffed veal complement the Christmas season. ❡ The roast can be made the day before, sliced onto a microwaveproof platter, and reheated later. The gravy can be reheated, too, and the desserts and appetizer made ahead and chilled. Only the salad needs to be tossed and the pasta cooked right before sitting down to eat. ❡ This works well as a buffet meal, but knives and forks will be needed for the veal, so you'll have to plan for at least small-table seating.

PREPARATION PLAN

EARLIER IN THE WEEK:
1. Make the truffles (see page 36) and refrigerate.
2. Make Christmas cookies.

1 OR 2 DAYS BEFORE:
1. Prepare the cheese dome and refrigerate.
2. Cook the veal and sauce.
3. Cook the pears; cool and refrigerate.

1 HOUR BEFORE SERVING:
1. Wash and dry the frisée for the salad.
2. Combine the salad dressing ingredients and set aside.
3. Put the water on to cook the pasta.
4. Slice the bread for the cheese and place on a platter. Serve with drinks.
5. Slice the veal and reheat with the sauce.
6. Cook the pasta.
7. Cook mushrooms after veal is heated and toss with drained pasta.

AT THE TABLE:
1. Heat the salad dressing and toss with the salad. Serve the veal, sauce, salad, and bread sticks.
2. Place pear and ice cream in serving dishes, garnish, and serve.

EVEN EASIER HINTS
Eliminate the pears and serve ice cream with truffles and store-bought cookies.

NUTMEG *Nutmeg is the dried seed of an apricot-like fruit that grows on evergreen trees native to the Molucca Islands, but can now be found in hot moist tropics throughout the world. The lacy red membrane covering each seed is mace, a spice often found in curries.*

BREAST OF VEAL STUFFED WITH PEPPERS AND BASIL

Serves: 6 to 8

Cooking time: 1 hour and 12 minutes to 1 hour and 22 minutes

1 (6-pound) breast of veal, boned and trimmed of excess fat (about 4 pounds boned and trimmed)

½ teaspoon coarsely ground black pepper

2 garlic cloves, minced

1 medium-size onion, finely chopped

1 tablespoon olive oil

2 red bell peppers, seeded and cut into ¼-inch strips

2 green bell peppers, seeded and cut into ¼-inch strips

¼ cup dry bread crumbs

¼ cup chopped fresh basil or 1 tablespoon dried

¼ cup chopped fresh parsley or 1 tablespoon dried

2 tablespoons grated Parmesan cheese

¼ cup tomato paste

½ cup beef broth

2 tablespoons dry white wine

Fresh basil, for garnish

8 plum tomatoes halved

Pasta with Mushrooms (recipe follows)

This attractive and inexpensive roast is delicious served warm or cold. We like to serve it at our tree-trimming parties because of the red and green peppers, but it is equally good chilled, in the heat of August, with dressed greens and crusty French bread. Here is our winter version of the menu made with extra sauce to serve over pasta.

If you make the roast in advance, slice and place on a microwaveproof platter and cover with plastic wrap to chill. Reheat on MEDIUM for 10 minutes. Heat the gravy, separately, on HIGH for 5 minutes or until boiling.

Pound the veal to an even ½-inch thickness, lay flat, and sprinkle with freshly ground black pepper.

In a 4-quart microwaveproof casserole, combine the garlic, onion, and oil. Cook on HIGH for 1 minute. Stir in the peppers. Cover tightly with the lid or plastic wrap turned back slightly on one side, and cook on HIGH for 6 minutes, stirring once.

Spoon the pepper mixture onto the veal, leaving a 2-inch border around the edges. Sprinkle with the bread crumbs, basil, parsley, and Parmesan cheese. Starting from the narrow end, tightly roll the veal and tie tightly every 2 inches with kitchen string.

Stir the tomato paste, broth, and wine into the same casserole. Place the roast in the casserole. Cover tightly again and cook on HIGH for 15 minutes; turn the roast over. Re-cover and cook on MEDIUM for 50 to 60 minutes or until tender, turning over after 20 minutes.

Let stand covered in the cooking dish for 15 minutes. (Letting the meat stand in the cooking dish lets the meat juices flow into the sauce and, in addition, the roast will brown even more.)

Transfer the roast to a serving dish. Skim the excess fat from the sauce and pour it into a boat. Remove the string and slice the veal into ½-inch-thick slices. Garnish platter with basil and plum tomatoes. Serve with the pasta, spooning the sauce over all.

ITALIAN CHEESE DOME

Serves: 6 to 8

Cooking time: Less than 1 minute

This light cheese mold, garnished with pungent dried tomatoes and green parsley, is wonderful for any Christmas gathering or Italian celebration any time, as it displays the colors of the Italian flag.

Combine the gelatin and water in a large microwave-proof mixing bowl. Heat on HIGH for 45 seconds to dissolve the gelatin; stir well.

Stir in the remaining ingredients except 2 tablespoons of the parsley, the 2 tablespoons chopped dried tomatoes, and bread. Line a 2-cup bowl or form with cheesecloth or plastic wrap and spoon the cheese mixture into the bowl. Cover and refrigerate for 3 hours or overnight.

To serve, unmold the cheese onto a serving plate. Remove the wrap. Sprinkle the dome with the chopped dried tomatoes and parsley. Surround with thin slices of Italian bread.

1 packet unflavored gelatin
3 tablespoons water
1 (15-ounce) container ricotta cheese
1 cup thinly sliced green onions, greens and whites
6 tablespoons chopped fresh parsley
½ cup plain yogurt
2 tablespoons lemon juice
½ teaspoon salt
½ teaspoon freshly ground black pepper
½ cup thinly sliced dried tomatoes plus 2 tablespoons chopped (about ⅛ pound) plus 2 tablespoons packing oil from jar
Italian bread, sliced

PASTA WITH MUSHROOMS

Serves: 6 to 8

Cooking time: About 15 minutes

1¼ pounds fusilli or other pasta
1½ pounds mushrooms, cleaned and cut
 in half
2 tablespoons unsalted butter
1 teaspoon lemon juice

Bring water to boil on top of conventional stove and cook pasta until al dente.

Meanwhile, combine mushrooms, butter, and lemon juice in a 2-quart microwaveproof casserole. Cook on HIGH for 4 to 6 minutes until heated through, stirring after 3 minutes.

Drain pasta and toss with mushrooms. Spoon into serving dish.

FRISÉE WITH WARM BALSAMIC AND PINE NUT VINAIGRETTE

Serves: 8

Cooking time: 3 minutes

2 large heads frisée or chicory, washed,
 dried, and torn apart (about 8 cups)
¼ cup olive oil
2 thinly sliced red onions
½ cup pine nuts
2 tablespoons balsamic vinegar
2 tablespoons Dijon mustard
½ teaspoon salt
½ teaspoon freshly ground black pepper

Place the frisée in a medium bowl. Set aside.

Combine the oil and onions in a 4-cup glass measure. Cook on HIGH for 2 minutes. Stir in the remaining ingredients, and cook on HIGH for 1 minute more. Toss with the frisée and serve.

242

SPICED POACHED PEARS WITH ICE CREAM

Serves: 8

Cooking time: About 20 minutes

8 firm ripe pears
2 lemons, quartered
1 cup sugar
½ cup dry white wine
2 teaspoons vanilla extract
8 cinnamon sticks
½ teaspoon freshly grated nutmeg
½ gallon vanilla ice cream

Keeping the stems intact, core the pears by cutting a cone out of the base with a grapefruit knife (this will help them retain their shape). Peel the pears and rub with cut lemon to prevent discoloration.

In a 3-quart microwaveproof casserole, combine the sugar, wine, vanilla, lemon quarters, cinnamon sticks, and nutmeg. Cook on HIGH for 3 minutes or until the sugar is dissolved, stirring once. Place the pears on their sides in the casserole, positioning the thicker ends toward the outside. Cover tightly with the lid or plastic wrap turned back slightly on one side, and cook on HIGH for 8 minutes. Baste the pears and turn them over. Cover again and cook on HIGH for 8 to 10 minutes or until tender.

Let the pears cool in their liquid, turning them over occasionally. Serve at room temperature or make up to 2 days in advance and refrigerate.

To serve, place a pear in each of eight serving dishes along with a cinnamon stick. Divide the cooking juices among the dishes. Add a scoop of vanilla ice cream and a grating of fresh nutmeg, if desired, to each.

DINNER
FOR A CRISP
FALL DAY

Serves 6

Mousse of Sole with
Cucumber Sauce

Boeuf Bourguignon

Buttered Egg Noodles with
Poppy Seeds

Baguettes

Pumpkin Clafouti with
Caramel Sauce

Mousse of Sole with
Cucumber Sauce

Boeuf Bourguignon

Buttered Egg Noodles with
Poppy Seeds

Baguettes

Pumpkin Clafouti with
Caramel Sauce

WINE SUGGESTION
Côte de Beaune

DINNER FOR A CRISP FALL DAY

When the last leaves fall and the winter skies begin to wrap the earth in a gray blanket, plan to serve this soothing meal. Stews, like this Boeuf Bourguignon are wonderful at this time of year, and all through winter for that matter. The microwave oven is perfect for this sort of stewed or braised dish because it doesn't have to be monitored much at all while cooking. Needless to say, the meat turns out beautifully tender.

PREPARATION PLAN

1 OR 2 DAYS BEFORE:
1. Make the mousse, but not the Cucumber Sauce, and refrigerate.
2. Make the clafouti and Caramel Sauce (see page 235) and refrigerate.
3. Make the beef and onions, but keep them separate; refrigerate.

EARLIER IN THE DAY:
1. Make the Cucumber Sauce (see page 89) and refrigerate.
2. Cook the mushrooms for the beef and refrigerate.

½ HOUR BEFORE SERVING:
1. Put the water on top of the conventional stove to cook the noodles (see page 45).
2. Reheat the refrigerated beef, combined with the mushrooms and onions. Cover and cook on HIGH for 15 to 20 minutes, stirring after 5 minutes.
3. Cook the noodles while the beef is heating.

AT THE TABLE:
1. Serve the mousse as a first course.
2. Serve the beef, noodles, and bread, with the wine.
3. Before serving the dessert, place the chilled clafouti in the microwave oven, if desired, and heat on MEDIUM for 3 minutes to bring to room temperature. Reheat the chilled Caramel Sauce on HIGH for 2 to 3 minutes or until heated through, stirring once.

EVEN EASIER HINTS
Instead of the clafouti, serve mint chocolate chip ice cream or pistachio ice cream (or both) with Caramel Sauce (see page 235), garnished with mint leaves.

POPPY SEEDS *The poppy plant whose seeds are used in cooking is in the same genus as the drug-producing opium poppy* (Papaver somniferum) *but of a different species* (hortense). *The tiny dried seeds are dark slate blue in color and add texture and flavor to baked goods as well as sauces for noodles, fish, and vegetables.*

MOUSSE OF SOLE WITH CUCUMBER SAUCE

Serves: 8 to 9

Cooking time: About 5 minutes

1 pound sole fillets
1 tablespoon (1 packet) unflavored gelatin
3 tablespoons cold water
¼ cup Homemade Mayonnaise (see page 155) or good-quality store-bought
5 tablespoons lemon juice
1 tablespoon chopped parsley
1 tablespoon snipped chives
1 teaspoon chopped fresh dill
½ teaspoon salt
¼ teaspoon freshly ground black pepper
Pinch cayenne pepper
1 cup heavy cream, whipped
Cucumber Sauce (see page 89)
2 bunches watercress
Dill sprigs, for garnish

If you are serving six for dinner, you'll be glad to have the extra servings for lunch another day.

Fold each fillet into thirds, in a two-fold-letter fashion, and place seam side down around the outer edge of a 9- or 10-inch glass pie plate, leaving the center open. Sprinkle with 1 tablespoon of the lemon juice. Cover with a paper towel and cook on HIGH for 3 to 5 minutes or until the fish flakes under the pressure of a fork. Drain the fish and finely flake with a fork.

In a large glass bowl, stir the gelatin into the cold water. Heat the mixture for 30 to 45 seconds or until the gelatin is dissolved; stir well. Stir in the mayonnaise, remaining 4 tablespoons of lemon juice, parsley, chives, chopped dill, salt, black pepper, and cayenne; stir. Mix in the flaked fish. Fold in the whipped cream.

Line a 9- by 5-inch loaf pan with plastic wrap and spoon in the mixture, spreading it evenly on top. Cover and refrigerate for 3 hours or overnight.

To serve, unmold and cut into 1-inch-thick slices (8 to 9). Place each slice on a dinner plate and arrange some watercress on one side and the Cucumber Sauce on the other. Garnish with a dill sprig.

BOEUF BOURGUIGNON

Serves: 6

Cooking time: About 1½ hours

The traditional stew of the Burgundy region of France calls for cubed beef to be simmered for hours with braised onions, sautéed mushrooms, and generous amounts of red Burgundy wine. We never intended to duplicate that one. This version is lighter and quicker, with a wonderful fresh flavor.

Place the bacon in a 3- to 4-quart microwaveproof casserole. Cook on HIGH for 2 minutes or until the bacon is limp. Add the onion, carrot, and garlic. Cook on HIGH for 2 to 3 minutes or until the onion is softened but not browned.

In a separate bowl, toss the meat cubes with the flour; add them to the onion mixture. Cover tightly with the lid or plastic wrap turned back slightly on one side, and cook on HIGH for 5 minutes. Stir in the seasonings, wine, and stock. Cover again and cook on HIGH for 10 minutes; stir.

Re-cover and cook on MEDIUM for 45 to 60 minutes or until the meat is fork-tender, stirring twice during the cooking. (At this point the stew may be cooled to room temperature, then refrigerated for a few days.)

Stir in the cooked mushrooms and onion. Cover again and cook on HIGH for 5 to 8 minutes or until the onion is heated through.

To serve, spoon onto a serving platter and surround with Buttered Egg Noodles with Poppy Seeds (see page 45). Sprinkle with the parsley.

NOTE: To reheat refrigerated Boeuf Bourguignon, stir in the cooked onion and mushrooms. Cook, covered, on HIGH for 5 minutes; stir. Cook on HIGH for 5 to 10 minutes more or until heated through. Remove from the microwave oven and let stand, covered, for 10 minutes.

2 slices (2 ounces) slab bacon, cut into ½-inch pieces
1 large onion, chopped
1 carrot, peeled and sliced
2 garlic cloves, minced
2 pounds rump or chuck roast, cut into 2-inch cubes
2 tablespoons all-purpose flour
½ teaspoon salt
½ teaspoon dried thyme leaves
½ teaspoon freshly ground black pepper
½ cup red wine
1 cup beef stock
Steamed Onions (recipe follows)
Lightly Sautéed Mushrooms (recipe follows)
¼ cup chopped fresh parsley, for garnish

STEAMED ONIONS

Serves: 6

Cooking time: 8 to 10 minutes

1½ pounds small white pearl onions (each about 1 inch in diameter), peeled
2 tablespoons water
½ teaspoon salt

In a 2-quart microwaveproof casserole, combine all the ingredients. Cover tightly with the lid or plastic wrap turned back slightly on one side, and cook on HIGH for 8 to 10 minutes or until tender, stirring halfway through. Remove from the microwave oven and set aside, covered, until adding to beef.

LIGHTLY SAUTÉED MUSHROOMS

Serves: 6

Cooking time: 3 to 4 minutes

1 pound small mushrooms, wiped clean and with stems removed
1 tablespoon unsalted butter
1 teaspoon lemon juice

In a 2-quart microwaveproof dish, combine the mushroom caps with the butter and lemon juice. Cook, uncovered, on HIGH for 2 minutes; stir. Cook on HIGH for 1 to 2 minutes more or until just tender. Set aside until ready to add to the beef.

PUMPKIN CLAFOUTI WITH CARAMEL SAUCE

Serves: 6

Cooking time: 18 to 22 minutes

1 tablespoon unsalted butter
1 pound peeled and seeded pumpkin, cut
    into ½-inch cubes
2 large eggs, beaten
¼ cup sour cream
¼ cup sugar
1 teaspoon vanilla extract
1 teaspoon grated orange rind
¼ teaspoon ground cinnamon
Caramel Sauce (see page 235; optional)

This "clafouti" doesn't brown like the traditionally baked version, but the unusual addition of pumpkin gives this dessert a golden glow and an all-american appeal. It is delicious whether served warm, at room temperature, or cold, and with or without Caramel Sauce! If you'd like to bring it to room temperature after it's been chilled, heat in the microwave oven on MEDIUM *for 3 minutes.*

In a 9-inch glass pie plate, combine the butter and pumpkin. Cover with wax paper and cook on HIGH for 4 minutes; stir. Cover again and cook on HIGH for 2 to 4 minutes or until the pumpkin is tender.

Meanwhile, in a small bowl, combine the eggs, sour cream, sugar, vanilla, and orange rind. Beat lightly with a wire whisk. Pour evenly over the cooked pumpkin. Sprinkle the top with the cinnamon. Cook, uncovered, on MEDIUM for 12 to 14 minutes or until the custard just sets, rotating twice. Let stand for 10 minutes before serving. Serve with Caramel Sauce, if desired.

ROUND-THE-KITCHEN-TABLE MEAT LOAF MEAL

Serves 6

Meat Loaf in the Round

Garlic Mashed Potatoes

Whole String Beans

Brandy-Walnut Sauce

or

Hot Fudge Sauce over Ice Cream

ROUND-THE-KITCHEN-TABLE MEAT LOAF MEAL

T his is a menu that we reserve for close friends and family. It is very comforting and delicious and informal, but not conducive to advance preparation. That's why you should only invite people who won't mind being in the midst of a bit of hustle and bustle. We usually don't serve a first course other than some carrot and celery sticks in a bowl while everyone is waiting for dinner.

PREPARATION PLAN

1 HOUR BEFORE SERVING:

1. Peel and cook the potatoes.
2. While the potatoes are cooking, mix and shape the meat loaf.
3. If time allows, assemble the ingredients for the dessert sauce, or do that right before serving.
4. Cook the meat loaf.
5. Meanwhile, prepare the beans for cooking.
6. Rice the potatoes and cover to keep warm.
7. During the standing time of the meat loaf, heat the milk for the potatoes.
8. Cook the beans.
9. While the beans are cooking, whip the potatoes and arrange in 6 mounds around the meat loaf (the warm milk makes them just the right temperature).

AT THE TABLE:

1. Spoon the beans in between the potatoes onto the meat platter. Serve.
2. Make the Brandy-Walnut or Hot Fudge Sauce (see page 49) while clearing the table. Spoon over ice cream.

EVEN EASIER HINTS

Eliminate the dessert sauce and serve a bowl of lovely fresh fruit.

GARLIC *Garlic is the bulbous annual of the lily family. The edible part is the root, and it is composed of small moon-shaped slivers called "cloves."* ❦ *From Greek and Roman antiquity to World War I, garlic juice had been used as an antiseptic to help in healing open wounds. But, of course, garlic is most noted for the wonderful savor it lends to Italian, southern French, and Spanish kitchens, although every cuisine is enhanced by its presence. A simple way to excite the taste buds of family and guests is to sauté a little garlic in oil; but make sure you're ready to follow rather quickly with a delicious dish.*

255

MEAT LOAF IN THE ROUND

Serves: 6

Cooking time: 16 to 20 minutes

1½ pounds very lean ground round
1 medium-size onion, finely chopped
½ cup dry bread crumbs
1 large egg, beaten
2 tablespoons chopped fresh parsley
½ teaspoon salt
¼ teaspoon freshly ground black pepper
1 (8-ounce) can tomato sauce
1 cup parsley leaves, washed and drained

This is one of our most requested recipes. We think it is probably because "man cannot live by fancy food alone" and the craving for a good meat loaf overcomes all of us sooner or later. It can be mixed, cooked, and served all on the same platter in only 16 minutes—the lean ground beef promises virtually no fat and very little shrinkage. It is wonderfully flavorful and moist.

Place the meat on a 10-inch microwaveproof serving plate with a lip. Make a well in the center and add the onion, bread crumbs, egg, chopped parsley, salt, pepper, and half the tomato sauce. Mix well and form an even round loaf that measures 6½ inches in diameter. Spread the remaining sauce evenly on top. Arrange the parsley sprigs in a wreath around the outer top of the meat loaf.

Wipe the exposed surfaces and edges of the platter clean. Cook, uncovered, on HIGH for 16 to 20 minutes or until done. Let stand for 5 minutes.

GARLIC MASHED POTATOES

Serves: 6

Cooking time: 12 to 16 minutes

1½ pounds potatoes, peeled and cut into
    1-inch pieces
4 garlic cloves, peeled
½ cup water
2 tablespoons extra-virgin olive oil
¾ cup milk
Salt and freshly ground pepper to taste

In a 2-quart microwaveproof casserole, combine the potatoes, garlic, and water. Cover tightly with the lid or plastic wrap turned back slightly on one side, and cook on HIGH for 10 to 12 minutes or until tender, stirring once halfway through the cooking. Let stand, covered, for 5 minutes.

With a slotted spoon, spoon the potatoes and garlic in batches into a ricer. Return the riced potato mixture to the same casserole; stir in the olive oil and cover. Heat the milk in a 1-cup glass measure on HIGH for 1½ minutes, until very warm but not boiling. Whip the milk into the potatoes with a wire whisk or hand beater. Add salt and pepper to taste.

To reheat, cover tightly and cook on HIGH for 2 to 4 minutes, stirring once.

PEPPER *Pepper is grown in the hot lands of India, Sri Lanka, and Brazil. Black pepper is second only to salt as the most popular seasoning used anywhere. We find pepper most flavorful when freshly ground. It adds a delicious dimension to almost every dish, from first course and salad to dessert. Try it when poaching fruits and add a little to pies and cakes.*

257

WHOLE STRING BEANS

Serves: 6

Cooking time: 3 to 4 minutes

1 pound fresh green beans, trimmed at the stem end but with points intact
2 tablespoons water
¼ cup sliced almonds (optional)

If your oven is large enough to hold a 12-inch round platter, these whole beans will come out perfectly without stirring. Otherwise, the alternate method will take a little longer.

Arrange the beans on a 12-inch microwaveproof platter with the points pointing toward the center (a few will overlap—these should be the thinner beans). Sprinkle with water. Cover with plastic wrap turned back slightly on one side, and cook on HIGH for 3 to 4 minutes or until tender-crisp.

Serve the beans as suggested with almonds, if desired, on the meat loaf platter.

NOTE: The green beans may be cut into 1½-inch pieces and cooked in a 2-quart microwaveproof casserole with ⅓ cup water. Cover tightly and cook on HIGH for 5 to 10 minutes, stirring twice. Let stand, covered, for 3 to 5 minutes.

BRANDY-WALNUT SAUCE

So simple, but everyone loves it!

In a 4-cup glass measure combine the brown sugar, butter, half-and-half, and corn syrup. Cook, uncovered, on HIGH for 2 minutes; stir. Cook on HIGH for 1 to 3 minutes more or until boiling.

Stir in the brandy and nuts. Cook on HIGH for 1 minute more. Spoon warm over ice cream.

Makes: 1½ cups

Cooking time: 4 to 6 minutes

⅔ cup dark brown sugar
¼ cup unsalted butter
¼ cup half-and-half
2 tablespoons light corn syrup
2 tablespoons brandy
1 cup coarsely chopped walnuts

TO SOFTEN ICE CREAM

1 Quart of Ice Cream: Place the carton in the microwave oven. Heat on DEFROST for 30 seconds to 1 minute or until soft enough to spoon easily. Spoon the ice cream into a large bowl and fold in any flavorings or other added ingredients. Spoon into a container that has a tight cover and refreeze for at least 1 hour to harden.

ECLECTIC AMERICAN

Serves 4

Corn Soup with Cucumber-
Cilantro Chutney

Oriental Scallops with
Vegetable Ribbons

Brown Rice

Chocolate Bread Pudding
with Lemon Sauce
or
Brownie Pie

ECLECTIC AMERICAN

*T*his menu is typical of *what many of us choose today when we go out to eat: A delicate first course, followed by a light seafood dish, perhaps with hints of Asian flavors and then the big payoff in a decadent chocolate dessert.*

The scallop platter is unique to the microwave because both vegetables and seafood can be cooked to perfection at one time.

262

PREPARATION PLAN

EARLIER IN THE DAY OR THE NIGHT BEFORE:

1. Make the soup and chutney, and refrigerate.
2. Make the Chocolate Bread Pudding with Lemon Sauce (cover and refrigerate) or the Brownie Pie (see page 116), covered and stored at room temperature.

45 MINUTES BEFORE SERVING:

1. Cook the rice.
2. Meanwhile, prepare the garlic and oil and the vegetables for the scallop dish.
3. During the standing time of the rice, sauté the garlic for the scallop platter.
4. Reheat the soup.
5. Assemble the scallop platter.

AT THE TABLE:

1. Serve the soup.
2. While clearing the soup course, cook the scallop dish and serve.
3. Place dessert on serving plates; serve.

EVEN EASIER HINTS

1. Cook the Brown Rice the day before and reheat it, or cook long-grain rice.
2. Serve ice cream with Lemon Sauce or Hot Fudge Sauce (see page 49).

GINGER *Fresh gingerroot, which grows wild in tropical rain forests of Southeast Asia and in Jamaica, was first cultivated in India and then made its way to China where it became popular as one of the five basic Chinese seasonings. The rhizome (root) of the ginger plant, it will impart a hot, spicy, yet sweet flavor to food. Crystallized and preserved, the root is considered a confection; dried and ground, it is used in baking (gingerbread) and in a score of main dishes such as Indian curry. ❦ The fresh root should be purchased as close to the cooking day as possible and stored in the refrigerator because spoilage is rapid.*

CORN SOUP WITH CUCUMBER-CILANTRO CHUTNEY

Serves: 4

Cooking time: About 25 minutes

1 tablespoon olive oil
1 medium-size onion, chopped
2 tablespoons all-purpose flour
1 cup chicken broth
2 cups fresh or frozen corn kernels
2 cups milk
2 teaspoons chopped fresh parsley
¼ teaspoon freshly ground black pepper
Cucumber-Cilantro Chutney (recipe follows)
4 cilantro leaves, for garnish

Combine the oil and onion in a 3-quart microwave-proof casserole. Cook on HIGH for 1 to 2 minutes or until the onion is tender. Stir in the flour to make a paste. Stir in the broth and the corn. Cover tightly with the lid or plastic wrap turned back slightly on one side, and cook on HIGH for 8 to 10 minutes or until the corn is tender. Stir in the milk, parsley, and pepper. Cover again and cook on HIGH for 6 to 8 minutes or until heated through.

To reheat from the refrigerator, heat on HIGH for 6 to 8 minutes or until the soup is heated through, stirring once.

To serve, top each bowl of soup with a spoonful of chutney and garnish with a cilantro leaf. Pass the remaining chutney.

CUCUMBER-CILANTRO CHUTNEY

Makes: About 2 cups

1 large cucumber, peeled, seeded, and finely chopped
¾ cup chopped fresh cilantro
½ cup plain yogurt
1 (1-inch) jalapeño pepper, seeded and chopped
2 tablespoons lime juice
½ teaspoon powdered cumin

Designed for the corn soup, this condiment is also delicious with grilled meats and scrambled eggs.

Combine all the ingredients in a small bowl. Chill until serving time. Can be refrigerated, covered, for up to 3 days.

ORIENTAL SCALLOPS WITH VEGETABLE RIBBONS

Serves: 4

Cooking time: 6 to 8 minutes

You will need a full-size oven that holds a 12-inch round dish to make this platter of vegetables in the center and scallops around the rim. You can substitute medium-size peeled shrimp for the scallops.

Place the sesame oil and garlic into the center of a 12-inch round microwaveproof platter. Cook on HIGH for 35 seconds.

Toss the peas, bell peppers, sprouts, and green onions in the garlic-oil mixture to coat well. Push the vegetables to the center, leaving a 2-inch space around the outer edge. Arrange the scallops around the vegetables.

In a small bowl, combine the soy sauce, ginger, orange juice, mustard, and cayenne. Spoon over the scallops and vegetables. Sprinkle the scallops with the sesame seeds. Cover with wax paper and cook on HIGH for 5 to 7 minutes, until the scallops are cooked through.

1 tablespoon sesame oil

2 garlic cloves, minced

½ pound snow peas

1 medium-size red bell pepper, cut into ⅛-inch strips

1 medium-size green bell pepper, cut into ⅛-inch strips

8 ounces fresh bean sprouts

3 green onions, cut into 1-inch pieces

1½ pounds bay scallops or sea scallops (if using larger sea scallops, slice into 3 pieces, crosswise)

3 tablespoons low-sodium soy sauce

1 tablespoon grated fresh ginger

1 tablespoon fresh orange juice

1 teaspoon Dijon mustard

⅛ teaspoon cayenne pepper

2 tablespoons toasted sesame seeds

BROWN RICE

Serves: 4 (3 cups)

Cooking time: About 35 minutes

2⅓ cups water
½ teaspoon salt (optional)
1 cup brown rice

Cooking brown rice in the microwave oven won't save you much time over conventional cooking, but it will be a fool-proof way to produce perfect rice that requires no tending at all.

Combine the water, salt, and rice in a 3-quart micro-waveproof casserole. Cover tightly with the lid or plastic wrap turned back slightly on one side, and cook on HIGH for 6 to 10 minutes or until the water begins to boil. Cook on MEDIUM for 25 to 30 minutes or until most of the liquid is absorbed. Let stand, covered, for 5 minutes.

LEMON SAUCE

Makes: 1 scant cup

Cooking time: 3 to 4 minutes

Juice of 1 large lemon, strained
½ cup water
2 teaspoons cornstarch
¼ cup sugar
1 tablespoon orange-flavored liqueur

Pucker up for this sauce! It will highlight either the Brownie Pie or the chocolate bread pudding or just about any ice cream or sherbet.

Pour the lemon juice into a 4-cup glass measure.
In a separate custard cup, combine ¼ cup of the water and the cornstarch. Add to the lemon juice, along with the remaining ¼ cup water, sugar, and orange liqueur. Cook on HIGH for 3 to 4 minutes or until boiling and it coats a spoon, stirring once after 2 minutes. Let stand for 5 minutes.

NOTE: You can get more juice from the lemon by warming it first on HIGH for 30 seconds.

CHOCOLATE BREAD PUDDING WITH LEMON SAUCE

Serves: 4 to 6

Cooking time: 15 to 21 minutes

1½ cups milk

4 ounces semisweet chocolate pieces

2 large eggs

½ cup sugar

1 teaspoon vanilla extract

6 slices good quality white loaf bread, ½ inch thick, cut into 1-inch cubes (about 4 cups)

½ teaspoon ground cinnamon

Lemon Sauce (recipe precedes)

Combine the milk and chocolate in a 4-cup glass measure. Cook on HIGH for 2½ to 3½ minutes or until the chocolate melts without boiling the milk, stirring twice.

Meanwhile, in a mixing bowl, beat the eggs and sugar together. Stir in the vanilla. Slowly pour the warm milk mixture into the egg mixture, stirring constantly. Pour the mixture back into the 4-cup glass measure. Cook on MEDIUM for 2 minutes, stirring once. Stir in the bread cubes. Let stand for 5 minutes, occasionally pushing the bread cubes down into the sauce.

Pour the bread mixture into a 1-quart microwave-proof glass or ceramic bowl. Sprinkle the top with the cinnamon. Cover with wax paper and cook on MEDIUM for 8 to 12 minutes or until a knife inserted 1 inch from the center comes out clean, rotating the pudding one-quarter turn twice. Let it stand directly on the counter for 10 minutes. Unmold, if desired.

Serve warm, at room temperature, or chilled right from the bowl with the Lemon Sauce spooned around the top outer rim, or spoon out servings onto each plate with a few tablespoons of sauce spooned on top.

Variation:

CHOCOLATE BREAD PUDDING WITH BLUEBERRIES: Stir 1 cup blueberries into bread-cube mixture right before cooking. Cook on MEDIUM for 12 to 14 minutes.

CELEBRATION MEAL

Serves 6

Mixed-Green Salad with
Large Garlic-Thyme
Croutons

Fish in a Bag Tied with a
Ribbon

Millet with Radishes and
Scallions

Cheesecake with Long-
Stemmed Chocolate-Coated
Strawberries

CELEBRATION MEAL

Serves 6

Mixed-Green Salad with Large Garlic-Thyme Croutons

Fish in a Bag Tied with a Ribbon

Millet with Radishes and Scallions

Cheesecake with Long-Stemmed Chocolate-Coated Strawberries

WINE SUGGESTION
Pouilly-Fuissé, sparkling Vouvray, California Chardonnay, or Champagne

The individually wrapped fish packets here are festive and would be appropriate for a birthday, anniversary, or other happy occasion. Each bag is untied at the table to unleash the fragrance of mint, tomato, and green onion. This meal opens with a green salad and crunchy herbed croutons made from a baguette, and closes with a creamy cheesecake and imperial-size strawberries that have been dipped in chocolate.

PREPARATION PLAN

THE DAY BEFORE:
1. Make the cheesecake and refrigerate.
2. Make the croutons and store in an air-tight container at room temperature.

EARLIER IN THE DAY:
Dip the strawberries and refrigerate.

1 HOUR BEFORE SERVING:
1. Wash and dry the greens for the salad. Refrigerate.
2. Make the millet and set aside, covered, until serving time.
3. Meanwhile, prepare the fish packets and refrigerate until time to cook.

AT THE TABLE:
1. Make the salad dressing and toss with the greens; serve with the croutons.
2. While clearing the salad plates, cook the fish packets. Serve with the millet.
3. Assemble the cheesecake with the strawberries and serve.

EVEN EASIER HINTS
For desserts, buy a celebration cake from a very special pastry shop.

MILLET *Probably some of the most "millet-wise" folk in this country are birds, for this tiny yellow bead is found in their seed. But we would do well to learn from a healthy bird, or the long-living folk of the Himalayas who consume this grain as their staple. Not only is millet nutritious (high in iron, calcium, phosphorus, and niacin), but it has an intriguing, almost nutty flavor and texture and is delicious as an alternative to rice.*

Although it never has gained any popularity in this country, it can be purchased in almost any health food store with the outer inedible hull removed. In other parts of the world, millet is pounded into flour for the Ethiopian bread injera *or the Indian bread* roti, *or simmered into a porridge in northern Africa. The Greeks, Romans, and Etruscans all made a porridge from it and it was one of the principal European grains in the Middle Ages.*

MIXED-GREEN SALAD WITH LARGE GARLIC-THYME CROUTONS

Serves: 6

Cooking time: About 5 minutes

24 Large Garlic-Thyme Croutons (recipe follows)
1 head romaine lettuce
1 head red-leaf lettuce
1 bunch watercress
1 small red onion, thinly sliced and rings separated
¼ cup olive oil
2 tablespoons red wine vinegar
¼ teaspoon freshly ground black pepper

Make the croutons and set aside.

Wash and dry the lettuce and watercress, and tear into pieces. Place the greens and onion in a medium bowl.

Combine the olive oil, vinegar, and pepper in a small bowl; whisk. Toss with the greens.

To serve, divide the salad among six salad plates and tuck 4 croutons around the leaves on each plate.

LARGE GARLIC-THYME CROUTONS

Cut the bread into approximately ¼-inch-thick ovals, to make 24 pieces.

Line the bottom of a 2-quart (12½- by 7-inch) rectangular microwaveproof dish with a paper towel. Place the bread on top of the paper. It will just fit. Cook on HIGH for 2 minutes. The bread should be dried (but not colored) at this point; if it is not, cook 30 seconds to 1 minute more checking carefully. Set aside.

Meanwhile, combine the oil and garlic in a 1-cup glass measure. Cook on HIGH for 1 minute.

Remove the paper towel from the dish and reposition the pieces of bread. Spoon the oil-garlic mixture evenly over the bread. Sprinkle with the pepper and thyme. Cook on HIGH for 1 to 2 minutes or until the croutons are crisp. (At this point you may place the croutons in an airtight container for up to 2 days.)

Makes: 24 (2-inch) croutons

Cooking time: About 5 minutes

2-inch-diameter baguette (if not available, use French or Italian bread and cut it in half lengthwise)
¼ cup olive oil
1 garlic clove, finely minced
½ teaspoon freshly ground black pepper
½ teaspoon dried thyme leaves

FISH IN A BAG TIED WITH A RIBBON

Serves: 2 to 6

Cooking time: See below

1 (4-ounce) flounder or sole fillet
1 tablespoon lemon juice
1 tablespoon dry white wine
1 teaspoon chopped fresh mint leaves
    plus 2 or 3 whole leaves
Pinch cayenne pepper
1 teaspoon unsalted butter (optional)
1 small tomato, cut into ¼-inch slices
2 mushrooms, thinly sliced
1 green onion, thinly sliced

The secret to the success of these individually wrapped fish is the fresh mint. The microwave oven allows you to tie the whole packet up with a ribbon (nonmetallic) for a festive touch, so choose a color to go with the occasion and your table.

Here are instructions for a single packet—make as many as you need.

Cut a 12-inch square of parchment paper. Place the fish fillet in the center, turning the thinner edges of the fillet under the middle to make a 4-inch-long piece. Sprinkle with the lemon juice, wine, chopped mint, cayenne, and butter, if desired.

Arrange the tomato and mushroom slices over the fish, overlapping them. Sprinkle with the green onion and top with the whole mint leaves (so that the aroma will come wafting out when the packet is untied). Pull all the edges of the paper together and tie with a ribbon about 12 inches long.

Place the packets in the microwave oven in a circle with a 1-inch space between them. Cook as follows:

2 packets	HIGH	3 to 4 minutes
4 packets	HIGH	6 to 8 minutes
6 packets	HIGH	8 to 10 minutes

NOTE: For doneness, open one packet and press fish to see if it flakes.

Each guest unties his packet to catch the first wonderful whiff. Eat right out of the packet and take advantage of all the wonderful juices.

MILLET WITH RADISHES AND SCALLIONS

Serves: 6

Cooking time: 20 to 22 minutes

Millet looks like birdseed (and actually is sold to feed birds), but what you will purchase in health food and some grocery stores has already had the hull removed. This is a wonderful grain and the flavor—well, try it for yourself.

Pour broth into a 2-cup glass measure. Heat on HIGH 3 minutes. Combine the oil, white part of the scallions, and millet in a 3-quart microwaveproof casserole. Cook on HIGH for 3 minutes. Stir in the broth. Cover tightly with the lid or plastic wrap turned back slightly on one side, and cook on HIGH for 8 minutes. Turn down power to MEDIUM and cook for 8 to 10 minutes until liquid is absorbed and millet is cracked and fluffy.

Uncover and stir well to allow excess steam to escape. Right before serving, toss with the lemon juice, scallion greens, radishes, parsley, and pepper.

Arrange the cucumber pieces on each plate in an overlapping semicircle. Spoon the millet next to the cucumbers, slightly covering them. Set the fish packets next to the millet.

1¾ cups fish broth or diluted bottled clam juice (1 8-oz. bottle juice + ½ cup water)
2 tablespoons olive oil
4 scallions, whites finely chopped, greens thinly sliced
¾ cup millet
1 tablespoon lemon juice
1 cup thinly sliced radishes
¼ cup chopped fresh parsley
¼ teaspoon freshly ground black pepper
1 English cucumber, unwaxed and unpeeled, thinly sliced crosswise

CHEESECAKE WITH LONG-STEMMED CHOCOLATE-COATED STRAWBERRIES

Serves: 6

Cooking time: 20 to 30 minutes

CRUST

¼ cup unsalted butter

1 tablespoon sugar

¾ cup zwieback crumbs

¼ cup finely ground walnuts

¼ teaspoon ground cinnamon

FILLING:

2 (8-ounce) packages cream cheese

2 tablespoons all-purpose flour

¾ cup sugar

2 large eggs

2 teaspoons vanilla extract

1 cup sour cream

6 ounces semisweet chocolate, chopped
    into ¼-inch pieces

6 large strawberries, preferably with
    stems attached

This cake looks beautiful perched on a footed cake platter and topped with the huge chocolate-coated strawberries.

To make the crust, place the butter in a medium microwaveproof bowl. Heat on HIGH for 1 to 2 minutes to melt. Stir in the remaining crust ingredients and blend. Cut two circles of wax paper to fit the bottom inside of an 8½-inch round microwaveproof cake dish. Place the wax paper circles in the bottom of the dish (this is essential for removing the cheesecake). Press the crumbs evenly on top of the wax paper. Cook on HIGH for 1 minute to partially set. Set aside; the crust will continue to set and harden.

To make the filling, place the cream cheese in a large microwaveproof mixing bowl. Heat on DEFROST for 3 to 4 minutes to soften. Beat until creamy. Add the remaining ingredients except the chocolate and strawberries, and beat until well blended and smooth. Place the bowl with the filling in the microwave oven. Cook on HIGH for 6 to 10 minutes or until very warm to the touch in the center, stirring every 2 minutes. (The mixture will be a little lumpy at this point, but it will cook into a smooth cake.)

Pour the filling into the crust, spreading out evenly on top. Place the cheesecake on top of an inverted microwaveproof cereal bowl in the microwave oven. Cook on MEDIUM for 8 to 14 minutes or until almost set in the center, rotating one-quarter turn once or twice. Let stand directly on the counter for 30 minutes.

The cheesecake will come out easily, but you'll have to turn it out and then turn it over again onto the serving plate. To do so, cover the top of the cheesecake with wax paper. Invert a plate on top and flip the cheesecake out onto the plate. Gently peel the wax paper from the crust. Flip out the cheesecake, crust side down, onto the serving plate. Chill for 3 hours or overnight.

To make the strawberries, line a plate with wax paper. Place the chocolate in a circle in a 1-quart microwaveproof bowl. Cook on MEDIUM for 2 minutes; stir. Cook on MEDIUM for 30 seconds to 1 minute more, stirring every 30 seconds or until melted.

Partially dip the strawberries into the chocolate, twirling to coat. Place the berries stem side up on the paper. Refrigerate for at least 30 minutes to harden. Garnish the outer rim of the cake with the strawberries right before serving.

ST. PATRICK'S DAY DINNER OR BUFFET

Serves 8

Irish Smoked Salmon Salad

Honey-Mustard Glazed
Corned Beef

Colcannon in Cabbage
Cups

Irish Soda Bread with
Orange Butter
or
Orange Marmalade

Irish Whiskey Cake

St. Patrick's Day Dinner or Buffet

Serves 8

Irish Smoked Salmon Salad

Honey-Mustard Glazed
Corned Beef

Colcannon in Cabbage
Cups

Irish Soda Bread with
Orange Butter
or
Orange Marmalade

Irish Whiskey Cake

❦

BEVERAGE SUGGESTION
Is there anything but a good
beer?

There is something about St. Patrick's Day that entices even the non-Irish to search out a meal from the "old sod." We find the event to be a great opportunity to serve visitors from abroad a bit of the Irish-American culture along with the meal. But because some of the traditional dishes can be lackluster, we have tried to bring them together in an unusual and exciting way. ⁋ As the guests walk in, they sniff a whiff of freshly baked soda bread, gilded with circles of orange butter. The first course of Smoked Salmon Salad is napped with a warm dressing enhanced by a whisper of dill. The corned beef gleams with a honey-mustard glaze and can be cooked in advance and served warm or at room temperature. Colcannon, the creamy potatoes, can be leisurely made ahead, warmed later, and served in cabbage leaf cups.

PREPARATION PLAN

THE DAY BEFORE:
1. Bake the cake.
2. Make the orange butter or orange marmalade.
3. Wash and dry the spinach and roll in a clean kitchen towel before refrigerating (or do this the day of the party).

UP TO 3 HOURS BEFORE SERVING:
1. Cook the corned beef, and let it stand in its juices until you are ready to glaze it.
2. Mix the salad dressing.
3. Mix the dough for the soda bread.
4. Prepare and cook the colcannon.
5. Make the glaze for the corned beef.

1 HOUR BEFORE SERVING:
1. Place the bread in the oven to bake.
2. Glaze and finish the corned beef.
3. Slice the butter and bread. Put the marmalade in a serving container.
4. Right before serving, heat dressing and toss with spinach. Arrange salmon on top.

AT THE TABLE:
1. Reheat the colcannon; serve the salad.
2. Clear the salad plates; spoon the colcannon into the cabbage leaves.
3. Slice the corned beef and arrange in the center of a platter.
4. If room permits, arrange the filled cabbage cups around the corned beef.
5. Sprinkle cake with sugar and serve.

EVEN EASIER HINTS
1. Substitute Smoked Salmon Canapés (see page 282) for the salmon salad.
2. Substitute Irish Coffee Ice Cream Cups (see page 289) and if desired, Irish Coffee Truffles (see page 288) for the Irish Whiskey Cake.
3. Use good store-bought white, light rye, or Irish soda bread instead of making it.

IRISH SMOKED SALMON SALAD

Serves: 8

Cooking time: 2 minutes

2 pounds spinach, washed and cut into 1-inch strips (8 cups)

½ cup vegetable oil

2 tablespoons red wine vinegar

2 tablespoons fresh lemon juice

4 green onions (white part only), thinly sliced

½ teaspoon salt

¼ teaspoon freshly ground pepper

1 pound thinly sliced Irish smoked salmon

2 tablespoons chopped fresh dill, plus 8 sprigs for garnish

Place spinach in a large bowl.

In a 2-cup glass measure, combine the oil, vinegar, and lemon juice. Add onion, salt, and pepper. Cook on HIGH for 2 minutes or until warm. Pour over the spinach and toss.

Place 1 cup of the dressed spinach in the center of each salad plate. Arrange the salmon slices on top of the spinach and sprinkle with chopped fresh dill. Garnish each plate with a dill sprig.

Variation:

SMOKED SALMON CANAPÉS: Eliminate spinach and warm dressing. Wash and trim 2 bunches of watercress. Thinly slice 1 loaf of black bread, and cut into canapé size. Cut salmon slices to fit black bread. Place 1 to 2 watercress leaves on each piece of bread, and top with salmon. Makes 24 to 30.

HONEY-MUSTARD GLAZED CORNED BEEF

Serves: 8 to 10

Cooking time: About 1½ hours

1 (5- to 6-pound) corned beef brisket, rinsed well
2 cups water
¾ cup whole-grain mustard
¾ cup honey
½ cup dark brown sugar
1 tablespoon prepared horseradish
¼ teaspoon cayenne pepper

This is delicious when served the first day or for days afterward as a leftover. We find that corned beef cooks most evenly when it is covered tightly with a glass lid, rather than plastic wrap.

Combine the brisket and water in a 4-quart microwaveproof casserole with a lid. Cover and cook on HIGH for 12 to 15 minutes or until the liquid reaches a rolling boil; turn the meat over. Cover again and cook on MEDIUM for 25 to 30 minutes. Turn the meat over again and cover. Cook on MEDIUM for 25 to 30 minutes more, or until fork-tender. Let the brisket stand, covered, for 10 minutes.

Meanwhile, combine the remaining ingredients for the glaze in a 4-cup glass measure. Cook on HIGH for 2 minutes; stir until well blended. Transfer the brisket to a microwaveproof serving platter, discarding the cooking juices. Spread the brisket with 1 cup glaze. Cook, uncovered, on MEDIUM for 10 minutes, basting twice with the juices. Let stand 15 minutes before serving.

Slice the corn beef very thinly across the grain. Serve warm or at room temperature. Spoon the extra 1 cup of glaze into a serving cup and pass with the corned beef.

NOTE: If the corned beef is cooked in advance, refrigerate it in the cooking liquid. To finish and glaze, first reheat beef in liquid, covered, on HIGH for 8 to 10 minutes or until boiling.

283

COLCANNON IN CABBAGE CUPS

Serves: 8

Cooking time: 16 to 29 minutes

1 large head cabbage
4 medium-size potatoes, peeled and cubed
½ cup milk
6 tablespoons unsalted butter
1 onion, chopped
½ teaspoon salt
¼ teaspoon pepper
4 green onion tops, thinly sliced

Colcannon is the name for creamy whipped potatoes that are studded with light green cabbage. Here they are presented in the palms of large cabbage leaves.

Wash and trim 8 nice outer cabbage leaves. Shred enough remaining cabbage to make 4 cups. Set aside.

In a 2-quart microwaveproof casserole, combine the potatoes and ½ cup water. Cover with a lid or plastic wrap turned back slightly on one side. Cook on HIGH 7 to 13 minutes, or until fork-tender, stirring once halfway through cooking. Let stand covered for 3 minutes.

Meanwhile, in a 1-quart glass measure, combine the milk and 4 tablespoons butter. Cook on HIGH for 1 minute; set aside.

In a 2-quart microwaveproof casserole, combine the onion and remaining 2 tablespoons butter. Cook on HIGH for 1 to 2 minutes. Stir into shredded cabbage. Cover with lid or plastic wrap, turned back slightly on one side, and cook on HIGH 7 to 13 minutes, or until cabbage is tender, stirring once halfway through cooking. Let stand covered for 3 minutes.

Mash the potatoes. Blend in the heated milk and butter. Add the salt and pepper to taste. Stir in the cooked cabbage.

To serve, spoon the potato-cabbage mixture into each of the cabbage leaves. Sprinkle with green onion.

NOTE: If making ahead and reheating, do not spoon colcannon into cabbage leaves. Keep in a covered casserole and reheat on HIGH 3 to 4 minutes, stirring once; then spoon into leaves and serve.

IRISH SODA BREAD

This is a relatively easy bread to make and bake in the conventional oven. We like to mix it up in the food processor, so we have kept the ingredient amounts to 1 loaf.

Preheat the oven to 400°F. Lightly grease an 8- or 9-inch cake or pie pan.

In the bowl of a food processor, combine the flour, sugar, salt, baking soda, and cardamom. Pulse the processor on and off a few times to blend the ingredients. Keeping the motor running, slowly pour the buttermilk into the mixture and process until a soft dough is formed. Remove the dough and work in the raisins, while kneading the dough six or seven times.

Form the dough into an 8-inch round and place into the prepared pan. Cut a large X that is about ½ inch deep on top of the loaf. Bake for 35 to 40 minutes or until the top is firm and lightly browned. Let stand on a wire rack for 3 to 4 minutes, before removing the loaf from the rack. Allow the loaf to cool at least 5 minutes before serving.

NOTE: You may make a sour milk substitute for buttermilk by adding 1 tablespoon lemon juice or distilled white vinegar to 1 cup of whole or non-fat milk. Let it stand for 10 minutes to sour and thicken.

If you don't have a food processor, combine the dry ingredients in a large mixing bowl, and then gradually mix in the buttermilk and raisins. Knead 7 to 8 times before forming into a loaf.

Makes: 1 loaf

Cooking time: 35 to 40 minutes

Shortening for greasing pan
3 cups all-purpose flour
2 tablespoons sugar
1 teaspoon salt
1¼ teaspoons baking soda
Pinch cardamom
1 cup buttermilk (see note)
1 cup raisins or currants

ORANGE BUTTER

Makes: ½ cup

½ cup unsalted butter
2 tablespoons orange juice
2 tablespoons grated orange rind

Place the butter in a small microwaveproof bowl. Heat on DEFROST for 30 seconds, or until soft. Stir in the juice.

To mold the butter, spoon it onto wax paper, forming a line down the middle. Sprinkle with grated orange rind. Roll the paper around the butter to form a 1-inch diameter log. Chill at least 1 hour. Slice and serve pats with Irish Soda Bread.

ORANGE MARMALADE

Makes: 2 cups

Cooking time: 15 to 19 minutes

½ pound seedless oranges, cut into paper-
    thin slices (about 1 cup)
½ cup water
2 tablespoons lemon juice
2 cups sugar

In a 3-quart microwaveproof casserole, combine the oranges, water, and lemon juice. Cover tightly and cook on HIGH for 5 to 7 minutes or until the orange rinds are tender. Stir in the sugar and mix well. Cook uncovered on HIGH for 4 to 5 minutes; stir. Cook on HIGH for 5 to 7 minutes more or until the bubbles reach the top of the casserole and the jelly sheets. Pour into sterilized jars. Refrigerate for up to 4 months.

IRISH WHISKEY CAKE

Coat the inside of a 10- to 12-cup microwaveproof Bundt dish with the shortening, making sure all the crevices are coated. Sprinkle ½ cup chopped pecans into the greased dish, turning the dish to coat all the surfaces very well and evenly. Set aside.

Place the butter in a large microwaveproof mixing bowl. Heat on DEFROST for 1½ to 2 minutes to soften, but do not melt. Meanwhile, sift the flour, nutmeg, baking powder, baking soda, and cardamom together in another bowl; set aside.

Beat the sugars into the softened butter until light and fluffy. Add the lemon and orange rinds and beat until blended. Beat in the eggs, one at a time. Stir in the yogurt and whiskey. Blend into the flour mixture. Fold in the remaining 2 cups pecans.

Pour the batter into the prepared dish and spread to make it even on top. Place the cake on a microwaveproof cereal bowl in the microwave. Cook on MEDIUM for 9 minutes, then on HIGH for 5 to 9 minutes or until the cake tests done. The top may appear damp but not wet; a toothpick inserted in the center will come out clean. Let the cake stand directly on the counter for 15 minutes. Turn the cake out onto a serving plate and let it cool completely. Sprinkle with confectioners' sugar and serve with coffee ice cream.

Makes: 24 servings

Cooking time: 16 to 20 minutes

3 tablespoons shortening or unsalted margarine
2½ cups finely chopped pecans
¾ cup unsalted butter
1½ cups cake or all-purpose flour
2 teaspoons freshly grated nutmeg
1 teaspoon baking powder
1 teaspoon baking soda
½ teaspoon powdered cardamom
½ cup firmly packed dark brown sugar
1 cup granulated sugar
2 teaspoons grated lemon rind
2 teaspoons grated orange rind
3 eggs
1 cup plain yogurt
¼ cup Irish whiskey
Confectioners' sugar

IRISH COFFEE TRUFFLES

Makes: 24 truffles

Cooking time: About 3 minutes

6 ounces semisweet chocolate pieces

2 tablespoons heavy cream

4 tablespoons unsalted butter, cut into 8 pieces

2 tablespoons Irish Whiskey

2 tablespoons sifted, unsweetened cocoa powder

24 coffee beans

Place chocolate pieces in a circle in a 1-quart microwaveproof bowl, leaving the center open. Pour in cream. Cook, uncovered, on MEDIUM for 2 minutes; stir. Cook on MEDIUM for 30 seconds to 1½ minutes more, or until melted, stirring every 30 seconds. Stir in butter until it melts. Stir in whiskey. Place the bowl in the refrigerator for 35 to 45 minutes, or until the mixture is stiff enough to roll into balls.

Meanwhile, line a cookie sheet with wax paper. Place cocoa powder in a small dish. Take 1 rounded teaspoon of chocolate mixture at a time and roll it around a coffee bean in a rough ball. Roll it in the cocoa and place on wax paper. Chill to harden. Store in a tightly sealed container in the refrigerator.

Serve with coffee, ice cream, or fresh fruit. Our favorite way is to spoon a good-quality coffee ice cream into 8 coffee cups. Place one truffle on the saucer of each cup and pass the rest.

IRISH COFFEE ICE CREAM CUPS

Whip the heavy cream and fold in the sugar.
Place 2 scoops of ice cream into each coffee cup. Spoon over 1 tablespoon Irish Whiskey and some sweetened whipped cream. Serve with a coffee truffle.

Serves: 8 to 10

1 pint heavy cream
¼ cup confectioners' sugar
½ gallon coffee ice cream
8 to 10 tablespoons Irish Whiskey

BOLD ITALIAN MENU

Serves 6

Linguine with "Roasted" Red
Pepper Sauce

Rolled Pork Roast with
Purple Olive Stuffing

Sweet-and-Sour Green
Onions

Mixed-Green Salad with
Large Garlic-Thyme
Croutons

Zuppa Inglese

Espresso

BOLD
ITALIAN
MENU

Broad strokes are taken with colors and flavors from the red pepper and basil sauce on the pasta to the tart olive-prosciutto-mozzarella stuffing in the pork roast. Accents of green onion grace the roast, and a classic molded Italian trifle, laced with whipped cream, ends the meal, along with espresso. The meal is served in the traditional manner with the salad after the meat course, but you may like to serve the salad with the meat course.

PREPARATION PLAN

THE DAY BEFORE:

1. "Roast" the peppers for the pasta sauce and refrigerate.
2. Make the croutons (see page 273) and store in an airtight container at room temperature.
3. Stuff and roll the meat and refrigerate.
4. Make the Zuppa Inglese; refrigerate.

2 HOURS BEFORE SERVING:

1. Cook the meat.
2. Meanwhile, put together the salad (see page 272) up to the final tossing with the oil and vinegar.
3. Prepare the green onions for cooking.
4. Boil water for pasta.
5. Unmold the dessert and decorate. Refrigerate again.
6. Ten minutes before the meat is finished, cook pasta.
7. When the meat finishes cooking, cover it with foil. Make the pasta sauce.

AT THE TABLE:

1. Toss the pasta with the sauce and serve.
2. While serving the pasta, cook the green onions.
3. Serve the meat with the green onions.
4. While clearing the main dish, toss the salad and serve.
5. Serve the dessert and espresso or coffee.

EVEN EASIER HINTS

1. Instead of the Zuppa Inglese, serve the Hint-of-Orange Custard (see page 136) with 3 orange segments on top and cookies.
2. Serve a simple dessert of fruit (such as grapes) and Bel Paese cheese instead of the Zuppa Inglese.

ROASTING PEPPERS *A roasted pepper is one that has had its skin charred over a fire or burner. The skin will rub off easily, which leaves a glistening, supple pepper which when sliced or pureed brightens up pastas, soups, or salads. ❦ But there is another way to peel a pepper, and that is by microwave. This method can produce the steam, between pepper and skin, that makes peeling easy, though without producing the roasted flavor. Otherwise the method works very well and leaves you free to perform other tasks while "roasting" takes place. ❦ For optimum results, the peppers should be cooked according to weight. One pound of the larger, rounder bell peppers works well, whereas ½ pound of the longer, thinner chili peppers is best.*

LINGUINE WITH "ROASTED" RED PEPPER SAUCE

Serves: 6

Cooking time: 15 minutes

1 pound linguini
¼ cup extra-virgin olive oil
1 garlic clove, minced
¼ cup unsalted butter
1 cup "Roasted" Red Peppers (recipe follows) or store-bought, cut into ¼-inch strips
2 tablespoons chopped fresh basil
¼ teaspoon freshly ground black pepper
1 tablespoon chopped fresh parsley

Bring water to boil on the stove and cook the linguini until al dente, or still firm to the bite. Drain.

Meanwhile, combine the oil and garlic in a 1-quart microwaveproof casserole. Cook on HIGH for 45 seconds or until the garlic is tender but not brown.

Stir in the butter, peppers, basil, and pepper. Cover with wax paper and cook on HIGH for 1 minute or until the butter is melted. Cover again and cook on MEDIUM for 6 minutes or until heated through and the flavors develope. Toss with the drained pasta, sprinkle with the parsley, and serve.

"ROASTED" RED PEPPERS

Makes: 1 cup

Cooking time: 16 to 18 minutes

1 pound (3 to 4) red bell peppers
1 tablespoon vegetable oil

Rub the peppers with the vegetable oil. Pierce both sides with a sharp knife. Place the stem ends to the outside of a 10-inch glass pie plate or 2-quart rectangular microwaveproof dish. Cover with a paper towel and cook on HIGH for 8 minutes.

Turn the peppers over; cover again. Rotate the dish a half turn and cook on HIGH for 8 to 10 minutes more or until the peppers are softened, slightly wrinkled, and the skins begin to separate from the peppers or blister slightly around the stems. Roll them in a kitchen towel to seal in the moisture. Let stand for at least 10 minutes.

Cut the peppers in half and remove the stems and seeds. With a sharp knife, and under cool running water, pull off the skins.

Variation:

"ROASTED" GREEN CHILIES: Follow directions above, cooking on HIGH 4 minutes on the first side and 4 to 6 minutes on the second. Makes ½ cup.

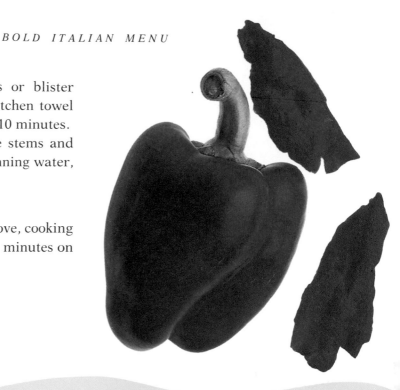

SWEET-AND-SOUR GREEN ONIONS

Serves: 6

Cooking time: 6 to 8 minutes

1 large unblemished lemon
1 pound (about 4 bunches) green onions
2 tablespoons Balsamic vinegar
¼ cup sugar
¼ teaspoon salt

Peel the lemon, spiraling it from the top to the bottom to produce 1 wide, long peel. Cut the peel lengthwise into quarters to form 6 long, thin strips. Set aside. Squeeze 1 teaspoon lemon juice.

Remove the tips and ends of the green onions and peel the outer layer. Divide the onions into 6 bunches, tying each with a strip of lemon peel. Arrange the bunches of onions in a 3-quart rectangular microwave-proof dish.

In a 1-cup glass measure, combine the 1 teaspoon lemon juice, the vinegar, sugar, and salt. Cook on HIGH for 2 to 3 minutes or until hot and syrupy. Pour over the onions.

Cover the onions with plastic wrap turned back slightly on one side. Cook on HIGH for 3 minutes. Rearrange the bunches from the inside to the outside. Cover again and cook on HIGH for 2 to 3 minutes more or until tender. Let stand for 2 minutes.

ROLLED PORK ROAST WITH PURPLE OLIVE STUFFING

Serves: 6 to 8

Cooking time: About 1¼ hours

3 pounds pork loin, cut lengthwise and butterflied
3 garlic cloves, minced
1 teaspoon salt
¼ teaspoon freshly ground black pepper
¼ pound thinly sliced prosciutto or smoked ham
8 ounces mozzarella, sliced into ⅛-inch-thick strips
24 imported purple or black olives, pitted
¼ cup pignoli (pine nuts)
1 teaspoon chopped fresh rosemary or ¼ teaspoon crushed dried
¼ cup white wine

Have the pork pounded (yourself or the butcher) to a ¾- to 1-inch thickness, making approximately a rectangle 10 by 12 inches. Remove any excess outer fat from the pork. Rub both sides of meat with garlic, salt, and pepper.

Lay the meat flat and arrange a single layer of prosciutto on one side. Top this with a single layer of cheese, and arrange 3 rows of olives close to the middle, leaving a ½-inch space along the longer sides. Sprinkle the surface with the pignoli and rosemary. Roll the meat tightly, beginning from one of the long sides. Fasten the roll about every inch with tightly tied string.

Place the pork roll into a 3-quart microwaveproof casserole that has its own lid. Pour the wine over the roast. Cover tightly and cook on HIGH for 15 minutes, rotating the dish once. Turn the meat over and baste. Cover again and cook on MEDIUM for 50 to 60 minutes or until the meat thermometer registers 170°F, turning the meat over and basting it halfway through the cooking. Rotate the dish two or three times throughout the cooking. Let it stand, covered, for 10 minutes before serving.

To serve, slice between the strings and untie each piece. Place on a serving platter that has been garnished with sprigs of fresh rosemary and basil. Serve hot or chilled.

NOTE: We find that this pork roll cooks much more evenly when covered with a lid rather than plastic wrap.

ZUPPA INGLESE

We suggest that you unmold this rum custard cake, which is similar to our English trifle, and garnish it with whipped cream and strawberries for a spectacular presentation.

Prepare the orange custard and let it cool.

In a small bowl, combine 1 tablespoon of the rum with the orange pieces and candied fruits.

Cut the pound cake horizontally into 3 layers. Keeping the layers together, cut the cake into twelve ½-inch crosswise pieces. In a 1½-quart bowl, arrange 1 layer of cake on the bottom and sprinkle with a little rum. Spoon a little orange custard and about 2 tablespoons of the orange pieces and candied fruit on top. Continue this process to fill the bowl, ending with a layer of cake sprinkled with rum. Cover the dish and refrigerate overnight.

To serve, whip the cream with the sugar in a small bowl. Loosen the cake with a long-bladed spatula or knife. Place a serving platter on top of the bowl of cake and invert it to turn it out. Fill a pastry bag with whipped cream and pipe from the crown to the base of the cake to form 12 to 16 segments. Pipe the cream around the base and at the crown, if desired. Decorate the base with strawberries.

Serves: 6

Cooking time: About 6 minutes

2 cups Hint-of-Orange Custard (see page 136)
5 tablespoons rum
1 cup orange segments (or other fruit in season), chopped into ½-inch pieces
¼ cup candied fruits
1 store-bought (11¾-ounce) frozen pound cake
1½ cups heavy cream
¼ cup sugar
Whole strawberries or other fruit in season, for garnish

HOLIDAY TEA

Serves 12 to 16

Cranberry Trifle
with Chocolate Holly Leaves
and
Sugar-Glazed Cranberries

Glistening Chocolate Pecan
Cake with Raspberry Sauce

Chocolate-Coated
Strawberries

Cinnamon-Spiked Truffles

Pine Nut Almond Cake

Raspberry-Oatmeal Bars

Pumpkin Bread Tea
Sandwiches

Spiced Nuts Under Glass

Mints in a Silver Bowl

Hot Spiced Cider

Coffee   Tea

HOLIDAY
TEA

Serves 12 to 16

Cranberry Trifle with
Chocolate Holly Leaves and
Sugar-Glazed Cranberries

Glistening Chocolate Pecan
Cake with Raspberry Sauce

Cinnamon-Spiked Truffles

Chocolate-Coated
Strawberries

Pine Nut Almond Cake

Raspberry-Oatmeal Bars

Pumpkin Bread Tea
Sandwiches

Spiced Nuts Under Glass

Mints in a Silver Bowl

Hot Spiced Cider

Coffee   Tea

*S*pread a table with *lemon leaves or greens and you have a background for this glorious table filled with cakes, tea sandwiches, and nuts for your guests. Chocolate Holly Leaves, crunchy Sugar-Glazed Cranberries, and truffles all add to the fun as edible garnishes.*

There are many ways to present these goodies, and we have described a few. Use your imagination and the illustration to give this menu your personal touch.

PREPARATION PLAN

UP TO 1 MONTH IN ADVANCE:

1. Bake the pine nut cake and the chocolate cake (see page 58), bread, truffles (see page 37), and bars and freeze.
2. Make nuts (see page 111) and seal well; keep at room temperature.

THE DAY BEFORE:

1. Make the Hint-of-Orange Custard (see page 136) and refrigerate.
2. Make the glazed cranberries (see page 136) and chocolate leaves (see page 137) and refrigerate.
3. Glaze and decorate chocolate cake, and make raspberry sauce.

EARLIER IN THE DAY:

1. Assemble the trifle up to final garnish (see page 135) and refrigerate.
2. Make Chocolate-Coated Strawberries (see page 276).
3. Prepare the sandwiches.
4. Combine cider ingredients, except rum.
5. Arrange the cakes on platters and garnish. The table should be attractively set. For the holiday season, we curve garlands of ivy or holly around the dishes on the table along with white and red flowers.
6. Twenty minutes before serving, add rum and heat cider. Brew coffee and tea.
7. Whip cream for pine nut cake.
8. Place chocolate leaves and cranberry garnishes on trifle.

PINE NUT ALMOND CAKE

Serves: 8 to 16

Cooking time: About 10 minutes

9 tablespoons unsalted butter

1 cup finely ground unblanched almonds

½ cup pine nuts

¾ cup sugar

2 large eggs

2 tablespoons Amaretto, or other almond-flavored liqueur, or rum

4 ounces bittersweet chocolate, grated

1 cup fine, dry bread crumbs

1 teaspoon baking powder

1 teaspoon grated lemon rind

¼ teaspoon cinnamon

Whipped sweetened heavy cream (optional)

Coat the insides, not the bottom, of a 9-inch microwaveproof or glass cake dish with 1 tablespoon butter. Sprinkle buttered sides with 2 tablespoons ground almonds to coat evenly. Cut a round of wax paper to fit the dish, using the outside of the dish bottom to measure. Place paper in the dish and sprinkle evenly with the pine nuts.

In a medium-size bowl, combine remaining butter with sugar, beating with an electric mixer to cream the mixture. In a separate bowl, stir together the remaining ingredients (except whipped cream). Add mixture to butter and sugar; mix well.

Spread the batter evenly in the prepared dish. Place the cake on an inverted microwaveproof cereal dish in the microwave oven. Cook on MEDIUM for 7 minutes, then on HIGH for 1 to 3 minutes or until the cake tests done, rotating one-quarter turn once or twice if necessary. (A toothpick inserted in the center should come out clean.) Let the cake stand directly on the counter for 10 minutes before turning out. Cut around the edges with a knife to loosen. Invert onto a serving plate and firmly tap the bottom of the dish to loosen; peel away the wax paper. Serve cake with sweetened whipped cream if desired.

NOTE: This cake freezes well and the flavor improves when tightly wrapped and refrigerated for a few days.

RASPBERRY-OATMEAL BARS

Makes: 16 bars

Cooking time: 10 to 13 minutes

¾ cup unsalted butter
1½ cups all-purpose flour
1 teaspoon baking powder
1½ cups old-fashioned rolled oats
1 cup dark brown sugar
1 (10-ounce) jar raspberry preserves

Place the butter in a large microwaveproof bowl. Heat on DEFROST for 1 to 2 minutes or until softened; do not melt. Meanwhile, in a separate bowl, combine the flour, baking powder, and oats. Beat the brown sugar into the butter until fluffy. Stir in the dry ingredients.

Press half the mixture into an 8-inch square microwaveproof cake dish. Spread the top with the preserves. Top with the remaining mixture. Cover the corners with foil to prevent overcooking. Cook on MEDIUM for 7 minutes; remove the foil. Cook on HIGH for 2 to 4 minutes or until the preserves bubble through the top, slightly, in the center; be careful not to overcook, since the cookies will firm up as they cool. Let stand on the counter until cooled, about 1 hour, before cutting into squares. May be refrigerated to speed the cooling.

PUMPKIN BREAD TEA SANDWICHES

Makes: 20 pieces

Cooking time: 9 to 11 minutes

1 recipe (2 loaves) Steamed Pumpkin
    Bread (see page 213)
1 (8-ounce) package cream cheese
½ cup Mango Chutney (see page 80)
1 dried apricot, cut in thin slivers

When the bread is cool (preferably the day after baking), cut into ¼-inch slices. With a 2½-inch round or fluted cookie cutter, cut each piece to make circles.

Place the cream cheese in a medium microwaveproof bowl and soften on DEFROST for 1 minute. Fold in the chutney. Spread onto the bread and garnish with dried apricot slivers. Arrange on platters and cover with plastic wrap to keep moist until serving time.

NOTE: You may use store-bought Mango chutney or apricot jam. Mix ½ teaspoon powdered ginger and ⅛ teaspoon cayenne pepper into the jam.

HOT SPICED CIDER

Makes: 25 (4-ounce) cups

Cooking time: 14 to 26 minutes

2 quarts apple cider
¼ cup brown sugar
2 lemons, studded with 4 cloves each,
**   sliced**
2 oranges, studded with 4 cloves each,
**   sliced**
8 cinnamon sticks
1 quart golden rum

Combine all the ingredients except the rum in a 4-quart glass measure or microwaveproof punch bowl. Cover with wax paper. Cook on HIGH for 14 to 16 minutes. Stir in the rum and pour into a punch bowl or simply ladle into cups.

SHORTCUTS TO BAKING

Even if you aren't planning much entertaining for this time of year, Christmas is still the time for baking. Here are some tips for how to make the microwave your "extra pair of hands" in the process.

BRANDY, FLAMED:
Pour ¼ cup liqueur (80 proof or more) into a 1-cup glass measure. Cook on HIGH for 10 to 15 seconds. Quickly pour into a large metal or glass ladle and ignite. Pour, flaming, over cooked cake or poached fruit. If you do not have a ladle, pour on the food and then ignite, but know that the additional liquid in the fruit may dilute the alcohol.

BROWN SUGAR, SOFTENED:
Place brown sugar in microwaveproof bowl. Add 1 slice soft white bread or an apple wedge. Cover tightly with the lid or plastic wrap turned back slightly on one side, and heat on HIGH for 30 to 40 seconds. Let stand for 30 seconds; stir.

BUTTER, SOFTENED:
Place 1 stick (½ cup) in a nonfoil wrapper on a microwaveproof plate. Heat on DEFROST for 30 to 40 seconds.

CHOCOLATE SQUARES, MELTED:
Open up the paper wrapping and place a 1-ounce square on a microwaveproof dish. Heat on MEDIUM for 1½ to 2½ minutes; 2 (1-ounce) squares on MEDIUM for 3 to 5 minutes; and 3 (1-ounce) squares on MEDIUM for 4 to 6 minutes.

CITRUS JUICE PLUS:
Get more fresh juice from 1 lemon, 1 orange, or 1 lime. Heat on HIGH for 30 seconds.

COCONUT, DRIED:
Place ½ cup freshly grated coconut on a microwaveproof plate. Heat on HIGH for 2 to 3 minutes, stirring each minute.

COOKIE DOUGH, FROZEN AND SOFTENED FOR ROLLING:
Form the prepared cooking dough into ¾-inch-thick, 4½-inch-diameter pancakes or 4½-inch squares; wrap tightly in plastic wrap and freeze. Unwrap and place on plastic wrap in the microwave oven; heat on DEFROST for 1 to 2 minutes to soften.

CURRANT GLAZE:
Spoon ¼ cup currant jelly into a 1-cup glass measure. Cook on HIGH for 2 minutes or until bubbling and melted. Stir before spooning or brushing onto tarts, cookies, or cakes.

LEMON OR ORANGE PEEL, DRIED:
Grate 1 lemon or orange, or peel into thin strips, making about 2 tablespoons peel. Spread out on a paper towel made for kitchen use or a paper plate. Cook on HIGH for 2 to 3 minutes or until dried but not dark, rotating the plate after 2 minutes. Cool and store in a plastic container in the freezer. Yields 1 tablespoon dried peel, which is double the flavor strength of the fresh amount when cooking.

(continued)

(continued)

NUTS, TOASTED:

Spread 1 cup nuts evenly on a paper plate or paper towel made for kitchen use. Cook on HIGH for 2½ to 4 minutes or until heated through, stirring every 2 minutes.

PECANS OR WALNUTS, SHELLED:

Combine 2 cups nuts and ¼ cup water in microwaveproof casserole. Cover tightly with the lid or plastic wrap turned back slightly on one side, and cook on HIGH for 1 to 2 minutes. Drain and dry before shelling.

PLUM PUDDING, WARMED:

Remove the plum pudding from its can and place on a microwaveproof plate. Cover with plastic wrap turned back slightly on one side, and cook on HIGH for 2 to 5 minutes or until heated through.

RAISINS OR DRIED FRUIT, PLUMPED:

Combine 1 cup fruit and ½ cup water, wine, or brandy in a microwaveproof bowl. Cover tightly with the lid or plastic wrap turned back slightly on one side, and on HIGH for 2 to 3 minutes or until softened. Let stand, covered, for 1 minute.

INDEX

THELMA SNYDER was born in Chicago but grew up in Connecticut. She holds a master's in Education from Hunter College, New York. Thelma is an award-winning oil painter who approaches cooking as she would a canvas. She now lives on Long Island with her husband, Dave, and their two children, David and Suzanne.

MARCIA CONE was born in Connecticut and grew up in New York and Pennsylvania. She holds a bachelor of science (Foods and Nutrition) from Purdue University and a certificate from Le Cordon Bleu in Paris. Travel is an avocation that she has pursued on six continents and it has been a major influence in her food tastes. Marcia is married to Koji Esaki and they live with their daughter, Hana, in Illinois.

Thelma and Marcia met in 1976 while working for a microwave manufacturer. In addition to writing cookbooks, they are featured monthly in *House Beautiful*, and have contributed to *COOK'S, Working Mother, Self, Redbook, Ladies Home Journal*, and other magazines.